Winter's Tales

NEW SERIES: 1

Winter's Tales

NEW SERIES: 1

*

EDITED BY

David Hughes

Constable · London

First published in Great Britain 1985
by Constable and Company Limited
10 Orange Street London WC2H 7EG
Set in Linotron Imprint 12pt
and printed in Great Britain by
REDWOOD BURN LIMITED
Trowbridge, Wiltshire

Reprinted 1985

British Library CIP data
Winter's tales – (New series/Constable; 1)
1. Short stories, English 2. English fiction
– 20th century
I. Title II. Series
823'.01'08[FS] PR1309.S5

ISBN 0 09 466600 8

CONTENTS

ACKNOWLEDGEMENTS

INTRODUCTION

Short stories need no introduction nowadays. There was a time, not long since, when literary fashion dictated that novels had the advantage. Not so. A good story, a few pages long, has just as big a world in it, as good a chance of letting the reader's imagination loose and of liberating his spirit at bedtime, when stories are best tackled.

The present volume is the renewal of a tradition that skipped only three years. Annually between 1955 and 1981 the house of Macmillan, under the gentle influence of Alan Maclean, issued a collection of Winter's Tales in time for Christmas, when long nights mean earlier to bed. The purpose was not only to introduce at a heartening moment some of the more promising beginners in fiction, but to offer at a choice season new work by old favourites. In launching this series Constable, one of the few remaining smaller and independent homes for authors in the making, have in mind the same mixture of fresh names and famous, a similarly exciting blend of themes and styles, to provide the reader with his own chamber music early or late in the evening.

There are ten stories here. They mirror vividly our world. So they all reflect one another. So there are more than ten different ways of enjoying their revealing distortions. But short stories, especially those as polished as these, need no introduction . . .

DAVID HUGHES

THE EXECUTOR

Muriel Spark

When my uncle died all the literary manuscripts went to a university foundation, except one. The correspondence went too, and the whole of his library. They came (a white-haired man and a young girl) and surveyed his study. Everything, they said, would be desirable and it would make a good price if I let the whole room go – his chair, his desk, the carpet, even his ashtrays. I agreed to this. I left everything in the drawers of the desk just as it was when my uncle died, including the bottle of Librium and a rusty razor blade.

My uncle died this way: he was sitting on the bank of the river, playing a fish. As the afternoon faded a man passed by, and then a young couple who made pottery passed him. As they said later, he was sitting peacefully awaiting the catch and of course they didn't disturb him. As night fell the colonel and his wife passed by; they were on their way home from their daily walk. They knew it was too late for my uncle to be simply sitting there, so they went to look. He had been dead, the doctor pronounced, from two to two and a half hours. The fish was still struggling with the bait. It was a mild heart attack. Everything my uncle did was mild, so different from everything he wrote. Yet perhaps not so different. He was supposed to be 'far out', so one didn't know what went on out there. Besides, he had not long returned from a trip to London. They say, still waters run deep.

But far out was how he saw himself. He once said that if you could imagine modern literature as a painting, perhaps by Brueghel the Elder, the people and the action were in the foreground, full of colour, eating, stealing, copulating, laughing, courting each other, excreting, and stabbing each other, selling things, climbing trees. Then in the distance, at the far end of a vast plain, there he would be, a speck on the horizon, always receding and always there, and always a necessary and mysterious component of the picture; always there and never to be taken away, essential to the picture – a speck in the distance, which if you were to blow up the detail would simply be a vague figure, plodding on the other way.

I am no fool, and he knew it. He didn't know it at first, but he had seven months in which to learn that fact. I gave up my job in Edinburgh in the government office, a job with a pension, to come here to the lonely house among the Pentland Hills to live with him and take care of things. I think he imagined I was going to be another Elaine when he suggested the arrangement. He had no idea how much better I was for him than Elaine. Elaine was his mistress, that is the stark truth. 'My common-law wife', he called her, explaining that in Scotland, by tradition, the woman you are living with is your wife. As if I didn't know all that nineteenth century folklore; and it's long died out. Nowadays you have to do more than say 'I marry you, I marry you, I marry you', to make a woman your wife. Of course, my uncle was a genius and a character. I allowed for that. Anyway, Elaine died and I came here a month later. Within a month I had cleared up the best part of the disorder. He called me a Scottish puritan girl, and at forty-one it was nice to be a girl and I wasn't against the Scottish puritanical attribution either since I am proud to be a Scot; I feel nationalistic about it. He always had that smile of his when he said it, so I don't know how he meant it. They say he had that smile of his when he was found dead, fishing.

'I appoint my niece Susan Kyle to be my sole literary executor.' I don't wonder he decided on this course after I had been with him for three months. Probably for the first time in his life all his papers were in order. I went into Edinburgh and bought box-files and cover-files and I filed away all that mountain of papers, each under its separate heading. And I knew what was what. You didn't catch me filing away a letter from Angus Wilson or Saul Bellow in the same place as an ordinary 'W' or 'B', a Miss Mary Whitelaw or a Mrs Jonathan Brown. I knew the value of these letters, they went into a famous-persons' file, bulging and of value. So that in a short time my uncle said, 'There's little for me to do now, Susan, but die.' Which I thought was melodramatic, and said so. But I could see he was forced to admire my good sense. He said, 'You remind me of my mother, who prepared her shroud all ready for her funeral.' His mother was my grandmother Janet Kyle. Why shouldn't she have sat and sewn her shroud? People in those days had very little to do, and here I was running the house and looking after my uncle's papers with only the help of Mrs Donaldson three mornings a week, where my grandmother had four pairs of hands for indoor help and three out. The rest of the family never went near the house after my grandmother died, for Elaine was always there with my uncle.

The property was distributed among the family, but I was the sole literary executor. And it was up to me to do what I liked with his literary remains. It was a good thing I had everything inventoried and filed, ready for sale. They came and took the total archive, as they called it, away, all the correspondence and manuscripts except one. That one I kept for myself. It was the novel he was writing when he died, an unfinished manuscript. I thought, Why not? Maybe I will finish it myself and publish it. I am no fool, and my uncle must have known how the book was going to end. I never read any of his correspondence, mind you; I was too busy those months filing it all in order. I did think, however, that I would read this manuscript and perhaps put an ending to it. There were already ten chapters. My uncle had told me there was only another chapter to go. So I said nothing to the Foundation about that one unfinished manuscript; I was only too glad when they had come and gone, and the papers were out of the house. I got the painters in to clean the study. Mrs Donaldson said she had never seen the house looking so like a house should be.

Under my uncle's will I inherited the house, and I planned eventually to rent rooms to tourists in the summer, bed and breakfast. In the meantime I set about reading the unfinished manuscript, for it was only April, and I'm not a one to let the grass grow under my feet. I had learnt to decipher that old-fashioned handwriting of his which looked good on the page but was not too clear. My uncle had a treasure in me those last months of his life, although he said I was like a book without an index – all information, and no way of getting at it. I asked him to tell me what information he ever got out of Elaine, who never passed an exam in her life.

This last work of my uncle's was an unusual story for him, set in the seventeenth century here among the Pentland Hills. He had told me only that he was writing something strong and cruel, and that this was easier to accomplish in a historical novel. It was about the slow identification and final trapping of a witch, and I could see as I read it that he hadn't been joking when he said it was strong and cruel; he had often said things to frighten and alarm me, I don't know why. By chapter ten the trial of the witch in Edinburgh was only halfway through. Her fate depended entirely on chapter eleven, and on the negotiations that were being conducted behind the scenes by the opposing factions of intrigue. My uncle had left a pile of notes he had accumulated towards this novel, and I retained these along with the manuscript. But there was no sign in the notes as to how my uncle had decided to resolve the fate of the witch – whose name was Edith but that is by the way. I put the notebooks and papers away, for there were many other things to be done following the death of my famous uncle. The novel itself was written by hand in twelve notebooks. In the twelfth only the first two pages had been filled, the rest of the pages were blank; I am sure of this. The two filled pages came to the end of chapter ten. At the top of the next page was written 'Chapter Eleven'. I looked through the rest of the notebook to make sure my uncle had not made some note there on how he intended to continue; all blank, I am sure of it. I put the twelve notebooks, together with the sheaf of loose notes, in a drawer of the solid-mahogany dining-room sideboard.

A few weeks later I brought the notebooks out again, intending to consider how I might proceed with the completion of the book and so enhance its value. I read again through Chapter Ten; then, when I turned to the page where 'Chapter Eleven' was written, there in my uncle's handwriting was the following:

> *Well, Susan, how do you feel about finishing my novel? Aren't you a greedy little snoot, holding back my unfinished work, when you know the Foundation paid for the lot? What about your puritanical prin-*

ciples? Elaine and I are waiting to see how you manage to write Chapter Eleven. Elaine asks me to add it's lovely to see you scouring and cleaning those neglected corners of the house. But don't you know, Jaimie is having you on. Where does he go after lunch?

– Your affec Uncle

I could hardly believe my eyes. The first shock I got was the bit about Jaimie, and then came the second shock, that the words were there at all. It was twelve-thirty at night and Jaimie had gone home. Jaimie Donaldson is the son of Mrs Donaldson, and it isn't his fault he's out of work. We have had experiences together, but nobody is to know that, least of all Mrs Donaldson who introduced him into the household merely to clean the windows and stoke the boiler. But the words? Where did they come from?

It is a lonely house, here in a fold of the Pentlands, surrounded by woods, five miles to the nearest cottage, six to Mrs Donaldson's, and the buses stop at ten pm. I felt a great fear there in the dining room, with the twelve notebooks on the table, and the pile of papers, a great cold, and a panic. I ran to the hall and lifted the telephone but didn't know how to explain myself or whom to phone. My story would sound like that of a woman gone crazy. Mrs Donaldson? The police? I couldn't think what to say to them at that hour of night. 'I have found some words that weren't there before in my uncle's manuscript, and in his own hand.' It was unthinkable. Then I thought perhaps someone had played me a trick. Oh no, I knew that this couldn't be. Only Mrs Donaldson had been in the dining room, and only to dust, with me to help her. Jaimie had no chance to go there, not at all. I never used the dining room now and had meals in the kitchen. But in fact I knew it wasn't them, it was Uncle. I wished with all my heart that I was a strong woman, as I had always felt I was, strong and sensible. I stood in the hall by the telephone, shaking. 'O God, everlasting and almighty', I prayed, 'make me strong, and guide and lead me as to how Mrs Thatcher would conduct herself in circumstances of this nature.'

I didn't sleep all night. I sat in the big kitchen stoking up the fire. Only once I moved, to go back into the dining room and make sure that those words were there. Beyond a doubt they were, and in my uncle's handwriting – that handwriting it would take an expert forger to copy. I put the manuscript back in the drawer; I locked the dining-room door and took the key. My uncle's study, now absolutely empty, was above the kichen. If he was haunting the house, I heard no sound from there or from anywhere else. It was a fearful night, waiting there by the fire.

Mrs Donaldson arrived in the morning, complaining that Jaimie was getting lazy; he wouldn't rise. Too many late nights.

'Where does he go after lunch?' I said.

'Oh, he goes for a round of golf after his dinner', she said. 'He's always ready for a round of golf no matter what else there is to do. Golf is the curse of Scotland.'

I had a good idea who Jaimie was meeting on the golf course, and I could almost have been grateful to Uncle for pointing out to me in that sly way of his that Jaimie wandered in the hours after the midday meal which we called lunch and they called their dinner. By five o'clock in the afternoon Jaimie would come here to the house to fetch up the coal, bank the fire, and so forth. But all afternoon he would be on the links with that girl who works at the manse, Greta, younger sister of

Elaine, the one who moved in here openly, ruining my uncle's morals, leaving the house to rot. I always suspected that family. After Elaine died it came out he had even introduced her to all his friends; I could tell from the letters of condolence, how they said things like 'He never got over the loss of Elaine' and 'He couldn't live without her'. And sometimes he called me Elaine by mistake. I was furious. Once, for example, I said, 'Uncle, stop pacing about down here. Go up to your study and do your scribbling; I'll bring you a cup of cocoa.' He said, with that glaze-eyed look he always had when he was interrupted in his thoughts, 'What's come over you, Elaine?' I said, 'I'm not Elaine, thank you very much.' 'Oh, of course,' he said, 'you are not Elaine, you are most certainly not her.' If the public that read his books by the tens of thousands could have seen behind the scenes, I often wondered what they would have thought. I told him so many a time, but he smiled in that sly way, that smile he still had on his face when they found him fishing and stone dead.

After Mrs Donaldson left the house, at noon, I went up to my bedroom, half dropping from lack of sleep. Mrs Donaldson hadn't noticed anything; you could be falling down dead – they never look at you. I slept till four. It was still light. I got up and locked the doors, front and back. I pulled the curtains shut, and when Jaimie rang the bell at five o'clock I didn't open, I just let him ring. Eventually he went away. I expect he had plenty to wonder about. But I wasn't going to make him welcome before the fire and get him his supper, and take off my clothes there in the back room on the divan with him, in front of the television, while Uncle and Elaine were looking on, even though it is only Nature. No, I turned on the television for myself. You would never believe, it was a programme on the Scottish BBC about Uncle. I switched to TV One, and got a quiz show. And I felt hungry, for I'd eaten nothing since the night before.

But I couldn't face any supper until I had assured myself about that manuscript. I was fairly certain by now that it was a dream. Maybe I've been overworking, I thought to myself. I had the key of the dining room in my pocket and I took it and opened the door; I closed the curtains, and I went to the drawer and took out the notebook.

Not only were the words that I had read last night there, new words were added, a whole paragraph:

> *Look up* The Acts of the Apostles, *Chapter 5, verses 1 to 10. See what happened to Ananias and Sapphira his wife. You're not getting on very fast with your scribbling, are you, Susan? Elaine and I were under the impression you were going to write Chapter Eleven. Why don't you take a cup of cocoa and get on with it? First read Acts, V, 1–10.*
>
> *– Your affec Uncle*

Well, I shoved the book in the drawer and looked round the dining room. I looked under the table and behind the curtains. It didn't look as if anything had been touched. I got out of the room and locked the door, I don't know how. I went to fetch my Bible, praying, 'O God omnipotent and all-seeing, direct and instruct me as to the way out of this situation, astonishing as it must appear to Thee.' I looked up the passage:

> But a certain man named Ananias, with Sapphira his wife, sold a possession.

And kept back part of the price, his wife also being privy to it, and brought a certain part and laid it at the apostles' feet.

But Peter said, Ananias, why hath Satan filled thine heart to lie to the Holy Ghost, and to keep back part of the land?

I didn't read any more because I knew how it went on. Ananias and Sapphira, his wife, were both struck dead for holding back the portion of the sale for themselves. This was Uncle getting at me for holding back his manuscript from the Foundation. That's an impudence, I thought, to make such a comparison from the Bible, when he was an open and avowed sinner himself.

I thought it all over for a while. Then I went into the dining room and got out that last notebook. Something else had been written since I had put it away, not half an hour before:

Why don't you get on with Chapter Eleven? We're waiting for it.

I tore out the page, put the book away and locked the door. I took the page to the fire and put it on to burn. Then I went to bed.

This went on for a month. My uncle always started the page afresh with 'Chapter Eleven', followed by a new message. He even went so far as to put in that I had kept back bits of the housekeeping money, although, he wrote, I was well paid enough. That's a matter of opinion, and who did the economizing, anyway? Always, after reading Uncle's disrespectful comments, I burned the page, and we were getting near the end of the notebook. He would say things to show he followed me round the house, and even knew my dreams. When I went into Edinburgh for some shopping he knew exactly where I had been and what I'd bought. He and Elaine listened in to my conversations on the telephone if I rang up an old friend. I didn't let anyone in the house except Mrs Donaldson. No more Jaimie. He even knew if I took a dose of salts and how long I had sat in the bathroom, the awful old man.

Mrs Donaldson one morning said she was leaving. She said to me, 'Why don't you see a doctor?' I said, 'Why?' But she wouldn't speak.

One day soon afterwards a man rang me up from the Foundation. They didn't want to bother me, they said, but they were rather puzzled. They had found in Uncle's letters many references to a novel, *The Witch of the Pentlands*, which he had been writing just before his death; and they had found among the papers a final chapter to this novel, which he had evidently written on loose pages on a train, for a letter of his, kindly provided by one of his many correspondents, proved this. Only they had no idea where the rest of the manuscript could be. In the end the witch Edith is condemned to be burned, but dies of her own will-power before the execution, he said, but there must be ten more chapters leading up to it. This was Uncle's most metaphysical work, and based on a true history, the man said, and he must stress that it was very important.

I said I would have a look. I rang back that afternoon and said I had found the whole book in a drawer in the dining room.

So the man came to get it. On the phone he sounded very suspicious, in case there were more manuscripts. 'Are you sure that's everything? You know, the Foundation's price included the whole archive. No, don't trust it to the mail, I'll be there tomorrow at two.'

Just before he arrived I took a good drink, whisky and soda, as, indeed, I had been taking from sheer need all the past month. I had brought out the notebooks. On the blank page was written:

Goodbye, Susan. It's lovely being a speck in the distance.

– Your affec Uncle

THE ATHEIST

James Chatto

On an afternoon in July, 1977, William Green was travelling south in a small aeroplane, en route from Bombay to Goa. The purpose of the journey, which had already brought him from London, was to eat a certain fish curry unique to the old Portuguese town. To this end, Green had fasted for forty-eight hours. At three pm the stewardess looked into the first-class cabin and gained the impression that her passenger was sleeping. He was, in fact, in the tertiary stasis of trance.

The fasts of a great gourmet have always been occasions of hushed reverence in the global kitchen. When Meissen Grosch prepared himself in this way all Vienna went tiptoe for days on end: the hooves of the cab-horses were wrapped in felt and the playing of the waltz forbidden by Imperial decree within a mile of the little house on Konstanzplatz, that no sound might disturb the concentration of the great man. In Paris also, though a hundred years earlier, it is said that Louis XVI was as sensitive to the delicacy of his friend and mentor Vicomte de Corse, even to the extent of outlawing the cooking of food over heat in the city during the time of vigil, lest any aroma corrupt the Vicomte's nostrils as he lay on his crimson day-bed in the Tuilleries. Indeed, so high was the King's regard for the master's powers of gastronomic discernment that when the old man finally died – poisoned, some maintain, by a spurned *patissier* – he commanded that his tongue and nose be embalmed in attar of roses and set within an ormolu shrine in the chapel at Versailles.

Alas, the relic was amongst the first targets of the Girondist mob in 1789, and the immortal organs have not come down to us.

Green however, and perhaps this is a measure of his greatness, disdained such external pressures. He relied on the ability of his own highly-trained and supple mind to prepare himself, coupled with an unchanging methodology. Whether he was staying at the time in his rooms in London, or in his hilltop cloister in the Tuscan countryside, he set about his fast with an almost impudent cool. Seventy-two hours before the chosen dish was due to be eaten, he would take from a box a single cigarette, unfiltered and made from a blend of harsh Balkan tobaccos rolled in the finest Moskott paper. This he would proceed to smoke.

Over the years, the timing of this heresy had become uncannily precise. For a day and a night following the cigarette his taste buds and olfactory nerves lay numbed and cataleptic. Like bees stunned by smoke, they had recoiled, stricken from their natural processes, leaving Green innocent of both taste and smell.

Such sensory silence was of crucial importance to the gourmet. Now, free of distraction, he was able to cleanse his imagination and carefully reconstruct his critical apparatus. First, he established anew the compass points of flavour – sweet and bitter, salt and sour; secondly, he lifted them into three dimensions, in the manner of an astronomer mapping the infinite night sky, readying his plan of reference for new phenomena; thirdly, and here his tremendous self-discipline was stretched to the full, he sealed all memory of everything he had ever eaten temporarily into the subconscious. In this way, when the time finally came to eat, his palate would be free of any association, of every link, however justified, that might disrupt the moment with an intimation of things past.

The last stage was a period of tranquil rest. While sensation returned to his nose and mouth, he would remain in semi-trance, holding back the tide of memory. Eating thus became a spiritual experience. While his body absorbed the colour, texture, sound, smell, savour of the food, his imagination led it into his naked mind, allowed its identity to permeate his pristine consciousness in an almost symbiotic ceremony. He became what he was eating, understood it as he understood himself, and only then, when the last plate was carried away would he awaken, as if from sleep. His eyes focused on the faces of those about him, his ears once again heard voices. Then too his pent-up memories were released in one adrenal roar to crowd around the new experience, comparing, questioning, pronouncing, finding the place for it to fit amongst his history. The taste reference structure was dismantled and stored away for future use, and the gourmet smiled, blinking in the applause of those who had eaten with him, and accepted a little coffee.

Green, then, was anything but haphazard where his vocation was concerned. Each time he was invited to eat some famous dish, some new creation, he set about it with absolute thoroughness, and because he was wise and aware of the danger of routine, and because he sought perfection and knew that it was not yet his, he embarked upon his fasting with an ever more profound concentration. Thus it was, as he lay back in the comfortable seat in the first class cabin, with the western coastline of India shimmering in the afternoon heat below him, that he first sensed the presence of the dish.

A moment before, Green had been on the point of entering the fourth stage of trance. His mind was naked and clean of all memory of taste and smell. It was as if he had never eaten in his life before, when suddenly he became aware of the imagination of food. It lay just beyond the womb of consciousness, like a word on the tip of one's tongue, a shape beneath the surface of mirky water, a ghost in the room. Green frowned: his initial reaction was that some thought of food had escaped from the prison of his subconscious, prompted perhaps by a chance aroma in the aeroplane, and he accordingly tried to force the fugitive back, not even bothering to bring it out into the light for study. But his memory would not accept it. He realised that the wall had not been broken. A flash of intuition: whatever it was was a fantasy, a will-o'-the-wisp formed by his ascetic mood, assisted no doubt by the altitude. It was not, thank God, that his grip was slipping, it was just a mirage, flitting across the desert of his hunger.

Amused, Green reached out to see what it was his mind had conjured, but the thing eluded him. And it continued to do so. For the remaining hour of the flight he played cat and mouse with the intangible taste and smell of the thing, chasing it around the solid frame of his graph of primary flavours, thinking he had it pinned one moment, only to feel it slip away again as he lunged. It was as if it were attached to him invisibly, a carrot before a donkey, never to be reached. Only it wasn't a carrot.

At the little airport near Goa a car was waiting to take him to the hotel where the curry was to be made next day. He remembered nothing of the drive, only dimly noticed the chefs and manager as they greeted him with low bows in the hotel lobby, smiling as he hurried by. In his room, he lay down on the bed and tried again in the helpful silence to reach the mocking phantom. He could not.

Green remained in his room for the rest of the day

and night and had still not emerged by the following morning. When the anxious manager knocked and said that the chefs were waiting to begin he told him that he needed further time to prepare his mind and body for the feast, and bade him deliver a crate of bottled water. The manager bowed and left, explaining that he understood; his brother was a brahmin and the importance of meditative renewal could not be denied.

The gourmet sank back onto the tortured sheets of his bed. The challenge of defining the thing within the brain was assuming the proportions of obsession. In all his life such a failure had never happened to him before. Here was a dish, a simple plate, he sensed, of something that his entire arsenal of critical gastronomy could not even approach. He calmed himself, drank a little water and set to once again.

Now he extracted with aching care a series of flavours from his memory and attempted to measure the phantom. The notion that it was something he had never before encountered was incredible, but the elusive ghost responded to nothing. It was like attempting to describe an entirely new colour, a colour not of our spectrum. If he could only make some tiny inroad, produce one faint echo ... After many hours he was forced to abandon the application of primary flavours as useless.

'This is absurd,' he muttered, startling the silence of his room. 'To be beaten, evaded, outwitted indeed by a flavour. I who am master of all flavours.' A small part of his mind now begged him to desist, to leave Goa and the fish curry for another time, to forego the chase. He ignored it with a look of repugnant disdain and turned his attention to the compound flavours. First he despatched the basic mixes into the void where the phantom lurked, mixes that were easily separable, like a fine sauce whose individual ingredients can be detected in each mouthful upon the spectrograph of the tongue. Then, the combinations that result from a more molecular merging, as in the unity of a blended whisky. Nothing led him the least bit nearer to the answer, no echo yet returned from where the presence waited, hovering in the darkness, beyond the edge of his understanding.

The days passed and he began to abandon altogether the tried and tested method of his science, but still he believed he would be able to explain the mystery if he could only taste the dish. Now he lunged at it wildly, or turned his back, then spun round very fast and dived into the darkness, but the phantom was no nearer. He found himself imagining that if he ran, hard and fast, he must eventually capture it. He ran.

So complete was Green's concentration that he failed to notice the symptoms of starvation as they seeped slowly through his body where it lay in that foetid little room. His stomach started to ulcerate and his abdomen was knotted with pain, but he paid them no attention. His already lean body grew weaker and more emaciated, but he was racing deep, in the benighted tunnels of his soul, pursuing.

He started to hear voices now: a thin high repetitious accent, intoning over and over again that this was the primal dish he was chasing, the first created union of two energies. Then there was the other voice, low and soothing, murmuring that it was in fact the last and final meal, the ultimate coitus of matter, the entrée of Armageddon. Both, he felt, as he hurtled on, were lies, and he dismissed them. *I will catch you*, he called, *and look upon you, taste and savour you, and know your origin. You shall not defeat me*.

Now as he ran, he formed new recipes, monstrous

and vile, and hurled them after the elusive demon: cocktails of sour and melting fat, salads of ash and turpentine, a glaucous compote of faeces and placenta. Not one fell even close. His breathless laughter mingled with his tears.

In another country perhaps he might have been saved; but the manager whose brother was a brahmin had determined that the great gourmet should not be disturbed until he wished to be. He too had read the diaries of de Corse and knew the value of the trance anticipatory. It was an accident therefore that led to the discovery of Green. A maid returning to work from a lengthy illness entered the room independently of the manager's wishes. She unlocked the door then stepped back gagging into the corridor, clutching her apron to her mouth. Green had been dead a week, of homeostatic dehydration. His weakened fingers could not open the bottled water.

Great surges of emotion swept his body with the violence of nausea: fear of failure, hatred for the unseen food and need of it, terror that it might disappear as quickly as it had come, leaving him alone in the great universe, and finally, at first quietly, then building up from the deepest bass until the sound of it filled him utterly, an all-pervasive adoration of the meal that stood beyond human description, impervious to the remotest understanding of mankind.

Let me see, he cried, *let me know. I am not worthy, but I would know you. I am your prophet and your vessel. Teach me. I love you.*

HE WHO SOWS HOPE IN THE FLESH

Gillian Tindall

Marianne was born and brought up in Brittany, on the rocky, seaward edge of France. She did not, however, come to value this fact till after her childhood was over.

Her family home was in Morlaix, which was too much of a town for her to grow up imprinted by the Breton landscape but too provincial to satisfy her latent taste for excitement and challenge. Encouraged by her easy-going, chronically bored mother, she spent her later childhood wishing she lived in Rennes, Nantes, or – why not? – in Paris. She still enjoyed the holidays organised by her father, when they climbed the gorsey cliffs to the west, and sailed and swam in the cold, blue Atlantic, and went on long walks between banks of stones and flowers to gaze at Celtic crosses. But after the age of twelve she enjoyed all this somehow absent-mindedly, automatically, her mind being fixed on a bright if vague future when there would be lighted streets and tall buildings and clothes and large cars and she would be greatly admired.

Since, however, the intelligence she had inherited from her self-taught father went on working whether she wanted it to or not, she continued to absorb with impatient ease the things he showed her, just as she also absorbed without effort her lessons at the Lycée. The distinctive crosses of Brittany, with their rows of troglodyte figures perched like birds, became familiar to her, as did the architecture of bone-houses and chapels. She particularly liked one bone-house – and long afterwards tried to remember where it had been, but by that time her father was dead himself so she could not ask him. It had had over its low doorway a Latin inscription – '*Quis spem carne seminat metet ossa*'. 'He who sows hope in the flesh reaps bones', she managed to translate eventually, while her father, who had left school at fourteen to become an apprentice in a grain business, stood by approvingly.

She also liked very much, and long recalled, a chapel somewhere in northern Brittany with stars on the blue roof that arched like a boat, and a Dance of Death round the walls. The faded fresco silhouettes, petrified in nods and becks and capers, trailing skirts and doublets, gowns and wimples, were each separated one from another by a skeletal figure: death himself, eternally replicated. Only one pair were not divided but held each other by the hand. They were (the elderly woman caretaker explained) the lovers: only love could vanquish death, by surviving it.

Marianne long kept these two messages, the Latin inscription and the Dance of Death, in her mind till, like much else of her childhood, they sunk away out of sight. But in any case they had always remained two separate experiences, two different stirring maxims about the impatiently awaited Life that lay ahead; it did not occur to her to analyse either message or to compare one with the other.

The messages remained in their appointed places as they had done for centuries, but time passed for Marianne and her wishes were granted. She went to university in Nantes, and afterwards to Paris to work as personal assistant to the director of a Public Relations firm. The work bored her, rather, and intimidated her secretly by its pointlessness, but Paris did not bore her and so she stayed. In any case there was no reason to return to Brittany. Her father had died while she was at

Nantes, her mother had remarried with what some of the family regarded as indecent speed and had gone to live with her new husband in another booming industrial town on the Loire.

Not till she was married herself – to Charles, an accountant with the firm that did the Public Relations firm's books – did she come to regard her Brittany childhood as being something that counted. And at first it reappeared in her consciousness almost superficially, like a new dress, or the house that she and Charles were buying, or the Louis Seize escritoire Charles's aunt had given them as a wedding present: the 'roots' she had abandoned without a thought turned out to be part of the necessary credentials for her married state.

It was Charles' doing; his own 'roots' were important to him, or so it seemed. At any rate he often referred to them. His family home was near a village in central France: a large, cold stone house with a small turret, dignified locally with the name of 'Château'. He had not, in fact, grown up there; it had been his grandparents' home, and now belonged to an uncle; but he had spent some holidays there as a child, and it was this place that surfaced in his memories, with lingering if patronising affection and nostalgia, as the location of childhood. In his reminiscences of morning wakings to the sound of *la vieille Marie* setting out hot chocolate on the terrace below, of fishing parties on the (small and gloomy) lake and of shooting expeditions in the woods, there was a hint of a social loss as well as a physical one, a suggestion of the one-time lord forced off his land by taxes and other unmentionable problems. But, as Marianne eventually realised, the family had had no money for the upkeep of the Château for most of the twentieth century, and Charles and she were actually more comfortably off now than he had ever been in his boyhood.

They lived in a distant but wooded and exclusive suburb of Paris. It meant a long train-journey each day back and forth for both of them, but (as Charles explained to their occasional visitors) it was worth it for the peace, the greenery, the views and the 'sense of retreat from the day's problems'. Charles was not the man to say to anyone, 'Of course we'd like to live in Paris but I can't afford the sort of flat there I would consider suitable to the figure I want to cut.' He did not even say it to Marianne, but she knew it to be so, just as she also knew, when she thought about it, that he enjoyed the day's problems, which made him feel important, and was actually rather bored at Roissy-sous-Emenonville at weekends. She also knew that while, in theory, he was all in favour of his wife 'having her own career' in the modern way (she was still a secretary but now with a women's magazine), in reality he would also have liked her to be at home all day ironing his shirts and preparing him elaborate meals. She usually managed, by hurrying, to catch an earlier train home than he did: he could become quite illogically annoyed if she were not there already waiting for him when he returned. He sometimes intimated, without saying so directly, that of course when they had a child she would stay at home: then, it seemed, her career would magically cease to be important. She never revealed to him that the thought raised in her a sense of panic. Sometimes now when she came home, tired and laden with shopping she had done in her lunch hour, and stepped into the shaded main room, where the Louis Seize bureau was polished once a week by a cleaning woman in her absence, she had the impression of stepping not into a place of retreat but into a cool, clean, silent tomb where she would one day be imprisoned forever. Perhaps a child – yes, one child, for he would surely say they could not afford more than one carefully brought up child and still retain their standard of living – would make all the difference? Perhaps. But she doubted it. Children grew quickly, didn't they, and went to school? She imagined a little boy like Charles, very keen on being top of the class, and her heart quailed. But at other moments she remembered herself and her father, long ago, ten years ago, in Brittany, and she took a little courage. Yes, a child would be nice and might, indeed, change everything.

But for the moment there was no child. At the Sunday lunch parties Charles was so keen on, and for which she toiled all day Saturday with a sense of suppressed but mounting exhaustion, Charles would talk about 'my wife's career', in a jocular way, as if it were a credit to himself both that she had one and that he did not object to her having one. At other times he would encourage her to talk to their guests about her childhood in Brittany: at first she could not think why. It wasn't as if he were *interested* in it, he never asked her about it when they were alone together. By and by it dawned on her, from words he let slip, that he thought 'real people', whether upper class or peasant (and preferably one or the other, not in between) had their roots in traditional country places. When she mentioned the cramped flat near the station in Morlaix rather than the cliffs and wayside shrines, he became quite annoyed and changed the conversation hastily.

In the holidays, in the interests of being real people, they usually stayed with the uncle in the Château at Merivalles. At first Marianne resented this rather. Merivalles, under the shadow of the Massif Central, was frequently wet and cold, even in August: it was also dull. It irritated her the way Charles would insist on leaving on Friday evening in the rush-hour the moment his holiday began, and drive tensely and nerve-wrackingly for many hours (he was a surprisingly bad driver and took foolish risks) merely so that they could arrive late and exhausted that night rather than the following day. What was the point of it, when then there was little to do each day for weeks?

After she met Daniel, however, her attitude changed. There was still, objectively, little to do. But from then on a sense of secret energy, comparable with Charles's tension but of different origin, infused her days at Merivalles.

Daniel was one of a number of men of roughly his own age whom Charles claimed to have been his 'childhood companions' and sought out each holidays. The village electrician, the café proprietor and several peasant farmers had drinks bought for them and were prodded into reminiscences of football and fishing. Marianne found Charles's heavy, would-be classless bonhomie on these occasions embarrassing. She suspected that several of these 'companions of childhood' had only the vaguest memory of Charles as a boy, and if they did not mock him among themselves that was because they were too amiable or slow-witted or simply did not care one way or the other. When Daniel Duclos, who was a local builders' merchant and was not often about the village, was finally introduced to her as another of the 'band' she surmised that he *did* mock Charles behind his genial, relaxed exterior, and at first resented him for this reason. But one day she encountered him on her own, in the square behind the church, and he put himself out to be friendly to her, asking her about her own childhood and where she had spent it. On an impulse, wishing to protect Charles from scorn but also to apologize for him and to separate herself from him in Daniel's mind, she said: 'My husband is always thinking of his childhood when he's down here. But of course you've lived here all the time; it's different for you . . .'

He said yes, it was different. Then, as if he too had an impulse to approach her, to establish what she was really like, he added: 'In any case, children, for me, return like the leaves in spring . . . Truth to tell, I don't see much connection between your husband and myself as children and who we are today. I feel more contact between myself as a child and the kids playing there on the green now. It's not individuals that count, for me, but life going on . . .'

'Of course you must be right', she said fervently. She wondered if any of the children she could see there playing now were his, and was going to ask, but he smiled and shook her hand and drove away in his lorry loaded with sand.

Later she discovered that he did have two children, but that he was separated from his wife, who had taken the children back to live with her own family in another village. He told her this when he delivered some roof slates at the Château early one morning (the roof underwent chronic but never adequate repairs) and she had invited him into the kitchen for a cup of coffee. Unusually, everyone else was out – Charles and the uncle and the uncle's apathetic wife had driven off to the local market town – and Daniel stayed with her in the kitchen for nearly an hour.

Later again, she heard from the café proprietor's wife, who was the village gossip, that Daniel was known to be 'one for the ladies' and that no one had been surprised when his wife had left. But by that time she was thinking a great deal about Daniel and interpreted the woman's cynical remarks according to her own needs and dreams.

It was that same holiday, wandering aimlessly in the neglected Château woods, that she came upon the little stone statue of the Virgin under an oak tree. She did not mention her discovery to Charles: she supposed he must know it was there, but she did not want to hear childhood reminiscences about it. The statue, she felt, was something for herself alone, a focus for her solitary walks. Next time she visited it, she picked a bunch of wild flowers for the Virgin as an offering.

Only as she was laying them across the Virgin's bare feet did it occur to her that it was usual, on such occasions, to make some sort of request. Of course (she told herself) she didn't believe in any of it; any belief she had had in God had faded away with her childhood: it was all just a matter of superstition and folklore, praying to a statue – but weren't superstition and folklore, in themselves, harmless and rather nice?

Stirred inwardly by feelings that had something to do with Charles, but perhaps more to do with quite other, recent movements in her life, she asked the Virgin to send her a child. Surely that, she told herself, was a harmless enough piece of traditional make-believe? And, who knew, it might even work.

Daniel called again, at the kitchen door of the Château. Only while she was preparing him another cup of coffee did it occur to her, with a sense of terrified delight, that he must have waited and watched to see restless Charles drive off unaccompanied, with his usual screech of tyres, before approaching the place. Uncle and his wife were in the drawing room which faced out the other way, over the bumpy lawns. This time Daniel had not driven his lorry up the drive but had left it, he said, on the other side of the woods. 'Come for a walk', he said. They went from the kitchen through the neglected vegetable garden and into the woods by the rusting side-gate. Among the dense trees, he took her hand. After a while she realised he was leading her towards the statue, and it seemed like a sign from the heaven in which she no longer believed, a miraculous answer to her prayers both voiced and unvoiced. The day was overcast, the woods were still: there was no one there but themselves, she had no fear of their being discovered or seen and nor, evidently, did he. Trembling, as they reached the grassy clearing where the statue stood, she wondered what words he would use to try to persuade her and whether he would expect her to resist . . . (Charles, before their marriage, had spent months elaborately seducing her, in such a way that she had realised that, if she complied too soon, he would be disconcerted and maybe put off. These days, however, he rarely took much trouble at all). It came as a shock, but also as a relief, when, as they reached the clearing, Daniel gripped her round the waist without a word and laid her on the ground.

'After all, *ma belle*, why not?' he said afterwards, as she lay in his arms still shaking a little with pleasure and fear. 'I wanted you: you wanted me. We both knew it, there was no point in words between us on the way here. Now it's done we can relax together.'

Tearfully she said: 'You won't despise me now, will you . . .?'

'Despise you? Why on earth? You were very nice. I'm already looking forward to the next time!'

'Well . . . Because I give myself to you so easily . . .' But even as she said it she recognised that in Daniel's terms the words were meaningless. He hugged her reassuringly and said: 'I told you last week: I don't have these sort of prejudices. I take people as I find them and do what comes naturally. I'm a cynic, if you like – but I hope I'm an honest one.'

In her mind she rejected the word 'cynic', thinking he was being self-deprecating. But the idea of his honesty and naturalness took root in her mind, possessing it as he had possessed her body; compared with him, everyone else, and Charles in particular, seemed unreal, hypocritical and afraid.

For the rest of that holiday she and Daniel met in the woods almost every day, and made strenuous love under the unperturbed gaze of the little Virgin. In a lovers' joke, they christened her *Notre Dame du Chair* – Our Lady of the Flesh. Marianne knew Daniel to be an unbeliever and supposed him to be simply unworried by the presence of the statue. Fundamentally innocent as she was, it did not occur to her to wonder if the watching Virgin added an additional element to the situation for him – or, indeed, if he had ever used this as a trysting place before. For herself, the statue imposed its own meaning on their meetings. Because of the way Daniel had presented himself in her life just after her request to the Lady, she told herself that she was allowing him to make love to her in order to have a child: it was five years now since she and Charles had got married and nearly three since they had stopped taking what Charles had always irritatingly called 'precautions', and they had both got anxious about the fact although they had hardly talked about it. Surely, even if God existed, He would (considering his own well-known prejudices) see a new soul on earth as a desirable end justifying the means? And anyway – she added to herself for good measure – Daniel was making her a better and more responsive wife to Charles, and surely God couldn't object to *that* either? The fact was that Daniel's frequent and prolonged attentions caused her to move through the days in a sensual dream, and when she abstractedly got into bed at night beside Charles he received the benefit of this. Also, feeling sorry for him, she was more solicitous of his comfort now, less easily irritated by him.

She needed these justifications, for she was trying not to know she was hopelessly in love with Daniel. He made it all too clear (such, she thought tenderly, was his honesty) that he was not in love with her. 'I enjoy you', he said easily. 'And I like lying talking like this afterwards too. It's nice to share bodies. And we have good times together, don't we?' She longed for him to say other things, but he never did.

The end of the holidays came. Charles, in spite of his proclamations about the need to return to one's roots and the essential reality of village life, was secretly bored and glad to return to the daily journeying between Paris and the suburbs. Usually she felt the same. This year, however, panic seized her: how could she bear to be separated from Daniel? The autumn stretched desolately ahead.

'Make him come down for shooting on Sundays', said Daniel. 'Some of the lads are getting up parties to go and beat the woods on the other side of the hill. There's lots of snipe there this year. He'll fancy the idea of that, won't he? I'll speak to him about it myself.' And evidently he did. Fancying the idea of it, Marianne thought, was just about right. Charles was an indifferent shot; he fell over tree stumps and jumped nervously at loud noises. And Merivalles was a long way to come from Paris just for a Sunday. But apparently Charles was so gratified to be invited on shooting parties by his 'boyhood companions', who had never shown such flattering interest before, that he was glad to make the exhausting trip again and again that fine autumn. And, as she had managed to establish the principle that she herself had taken to solitary country walks as a means of relaxation from 'the nervous tension of her career', she always came too.

Now, she and Daniel did not invariably meet by Our Lady of the Flesh. Some Sundays, fearing to be spotted in the woods by other shooting parties (or, worse, by Charles himself!) Daniel would lead her to other hidden places. Taking her hand and pulling her behind him, as he had done that first time, drawing her onwards like the lover in the fresco whom even death cannot separate from his dear one, he took her to shadowy barns full of straw, or derelict cottages where they gasped out their pleasure on cracked tiled floors among broken sticks of furniture, chinks of light filtering onto their partially-clothed bodies through sagging roof-tiles. But always, in her mind, the Virgin in the woods presided over their coupling. Surely, surely, she thought – clinging to her great excuse – she would become pregnant soon, now that her body was so imbued with Daniel's vital one? Once, at the end of October, she believed it had happened, but it turned out to be a false hope.

Daniel, when she confided her great wish to him, was as sanguine about the prospect as he was about everything else. 'Why not?' he said. 'Your husband would think it was his, I suppose?' She nodded. 'I've two children by my wife and another by a girl near Châteaumeillant', he went on. 'And I believe I may have left several in the south where I did my military service. Why not you too?'

It was lucky, she tried to tell herself, that he took it like this, so matter-of-factly and naturally . . . But she could not help minding terribly that a child between them, which for her would symbolise an eternal link which even death would not sever, to him apparently had no significance at all. In any case he simply would not discuss the future, even the near future. When, daunted by the thought of the approaching winter of separation, when she would have little or no excuse to make the journey to Merivalles, she tried to talk hopefully of next spring, he just laughed and said, 'Well, let's see when the time comes.' The thought that by then his naturalness and matter-of-factness might have led him to another partner, another body to lie with under the cool gaze of the Virgin as next year's buds swelled, was one she could not bear even to think. Surely nothing as terrible as that could happen? Surely Daniel himself must value – a bit – what she valued so desperately . . . And anyway, perhaps by next spring she would be expecting his child.

An odd thing was happening these days in her feelings for Charles. In the summer, enveloped in her sensual dream, she had hardly thought of him at all, but now, as the weeks stretched ahead and the weather grew colder, she found herself turning to him more, relying on him more for the security and comfort she could no longer find within herself. Except for the increasingly rare hours she spent in Daniel's arms, and the day or two of anticipation before, she was unhappy most of the time now. Life seemed so fragile and sketchy, the future so unsure, and she herself rooted in so very little. She thought of her father sometimes, and how they had belonged together and how she might never belong anywhere again, and sometimes she cried.

Occasionally Daniel had asked her, 'He doesn't suspect anything, does he?' and she always answered no. At first, in the happy summer, insulated by the spell of the flesh, she had not cared if Charles found out about her and Daniel or not. Now, in her dread and loneliness, she too felt that it was important he should never know. For if Charles rejected her what – and where – would she have left? No one and nowhere. She might as well not exist.

Near Christmas, when she had not seen Daniel for nearly a month, the uncle's wife providentially fell ill, and she was able to suggest to Charles that they spend their New Year holiday there. He seemed touched and pleased that she should show so much family feeling for his relations, and though she thought him a fool she also warmed to him. It was true what people sometimes (rather dubiously) said: Charles had many qualities. That night she cried wordlessly on his shoulder, and later, for the first time, he asked her if she wouldn't like to consult a gynaecologist to 'see if that would do the trick and start a kiddie'. He even offered to go with her. Knowing how much such a tacit admission of possible failure in himself must cost him, she felt very tenderly towards him.

Two days after New Years Day, she met Daniel by arrangement in the woods. The place was transformed as if by a theatrical device. The lattice of bare branches and twigs was covered in a hoar frost that the pallid winter sun had not even managed to melt. A frozen white alley led to the Lady, as if into an enchanted grotto. Her calm, uninvolved expression was just the same, but a strand of cobweb across her head and shoulders had been transformed by frost into a lace mantilla.

'We must be mad', said Daniel, cheerfully but impatiently, as they fumbled about under each other's layers of clothes. He had brought a rug with him for them to lie on, but it crackled under them on frozen leaves, and even she had to admit that it was almost unbearably cold. Did Daniel even mean to make love to her this time? She was not sure.

With his hand half-heartedly on her breast, under her jersey, he asked suddenly:

'Where's your husband, then? Doesn't he think it odd you're out so long on such a day?'

'He's gone to the butchers in Gueret. He'll be back soon, I think. I musn't stay here long today.' She felt so desolate at the thought, and at the fact that Daniel didn't seem particularly disappointed, that the idea of Charles' return with lamb chops and the newspaper was almost comforting.

Trying to distract both herself and Daniel from this new, terrible discomfort and awkwardness, she suddenly asked him if he knew the origin of the Virgin. 'Had there' – she asked tremulously – 'been a fertility cult in this wood in the olden days?'

He stared at her and then laughed.

'Why no – I thought you knew. Hasn't your husband or his family told you?'

'Told me what?'

'Well it's an old story, but not that old. Someone in your husband's family – a great uncle or cousin of that generation I suppose it would have been – was climbing that big elm over there when he was a boy to get at a magpie's nest. He fell from the tree and was killed. His family put the statue up in memory of him. About – oh, some time before the First World War, I suppose that would have been. Look at the base of the plinth, there where the leaves cover it – his name's there and an inscription.' He laughed again, but as if uneasy without his usual good humour. 'I thought you knew', he repeated, as if excusing himself for something.

Our Lady of the Flesh . . .

In the silence that followed she said at last, in a small voice: 'It's no laughing matter, surely.'

'Too right', he agreed equably, and got to his feet. Evidently they were not to enjoy each other's bodies, that day.

She accompanied him back to where he had left his lorry parked by the side of a little-frequented lane. 'Oh do drive carefully', she said with sudden fear. The roads were icy, but it was really the story he had just told her that filled her with superstitious dread.

'Of course I will. You know me – I've a charmed life. Well: till the next time, *ma belle* –' He hugged her with his habitual, cynical warmth and freedom from all emotion, and drove away.

Walking slowly back up the bumpy drive of the Château she imagined his lorry at the foot of some frosty ravine, and thought with an obsessive misery in which there was even some hint of relief, 'I may never see him again'.

He who sows hope in the flesh reaps bones.

But it was not Daniel's lorry that ended in a ravine that day.

At roughly the same moment that she and Daniel were saying goodbye, Charles, with lamb-chops, newspaper and a bottle of claret on the seat beside him, took a bend in the road with his usual rather excessive verve. The bottle rolled off the seat, he swore, braked, took his eyes from the road for a moment – and then everything happened at once: screeching tyres, a lop-sided vista of white branches, a wheeling sky, a crunching noise, a violent bouncing, breaking glass, crackling frost, slashing twigs, a searing pain, falling, rolling, blackness . . . And, at long last, silence.

The silence prolonged itself.

MOKUSEI: A LOVE STORY

Cees Nooteboom

Translated from the Dutch by Adrienne Dixon

How hard – to make ashes of the mind.

Sugawara no Michizane, 9th century

1

The photographer, still a young man and in his early thirties, very Dutch in appearance, was walking along a busy shopping street in the Ginza. He was thinking of the photograph he would have liked to take. It was late evening and he felt the chill of the early, northerly fall. The cool air, perhaps coming from the sea, imparted something rural to the atmosphere, and God knows, maybe this was the reason why he succeeded in not letting the barbarity of his surroundings affect him and thus retained the vision of the woman he would have liked to photograph. His name was Arnold Pessers and he was in Japan for the fifth time. And it was the last, he knew. He also knew that if he were to pay attention to what was around him, he would be filled with hate, a hate he would not have considered possible on his first visit. Japan, he thought, had taken Japan away from him. The two Japans, in which the Japanese themselves moved about so apparently noiselessly and unperturbedly – until someone like Mishima broke the fiction with a flagrant, reckless suicide – had also split him in two, into banalities such as love and hate. This country, these two countries, would never be his. That in itself did not matter so much, but it had also turned against him, with the shattering force of a luckless love affair, so that even his own love had changed into hate. The first time he had said something to this effect, to his friend De Goede, who had been attached to the Cultural Section at the Belgian Embassy for four years, De Goede had laughed in his face. That had been at the time of his first doubts, as long ago as that.

'There are no two Japans, certainly not to the Japanese. To them it is indivisible, if they think about it at all. You have come here, like everyone else, on false pretences. I have seen it all too often. They've read a book by Tanizaki, or maybe they've seen *Shogun*, a Hiroshige exhibition, they've picked up a few half-baked ideas about Zen, and they think they know all about it. It is one big misunderstanding, literally, a mis-understanding. I can always pick them out at once, I only have to have lunch with them. You can't say they are boasting exactly, but they always want you to know that they know the score, that they are old hands, even before they've ever set foot in the place. *Sashimi, suimono, mizutaki*, the words come tripping out of their mouths as if they had never eaten anything else, they practised in Amsterdam at the Okura or at Kyo's, it wouldn't surprise me. Usually they are also very happy here, the first time, provided you organize things properly for them. They want aesthetics, so all Hondas have to be made invisible. They refuse to see the vulgarity, which is what three quarters of life consists of, here as much as anywhere else, and that is what you have to help them with. So, not too long in Tokyo, but straightaway to Nikko or by bullet train – oh yes, they want that all right – to Kyoto, no messing about. They insist on sleeping in a genuine *ryokan*, on sitting in a wooden tub with a whole family, they spend long hours in the Kabuki-za and pretend they understand it, visit a monastery if at all possible, where they then find confirmation of their notions about the spirituality of Japan. What they are looking for is a Netherlands where everyone knows Lanceloet by heart, or a Flanders consisting of nothing but Memlinc, the city centre of Bruges and the finer points of Ruusbroec. Such countries exist only in time, they haven't existed in space for goodness knows how long.

Arnold Pessers remembered exactly when this conversation had taken place, or rather, he remembered the day, though not the year. The Emperor's birthday had apparently been of such mystical significance that the number of the year in which it occurred hardly mattered. He could see it again now. They were standing together in a long line of Japanese, in front of the superhumanly tall gates of the Imperial Palace. The divine presence, so it was said, had already manifested itself in a window two times that day, and it was not certain whether it would appear again. Officers with swords continually straightened the line. Peering past the sharp of their swords as though an enemy were approaching on the horizon, they drew an imaginary rope alongside the crowd; any protruding elbow would be hacked off. Arnold Pessers thought of a photograph he had once seen, of a Japanese soldier about to behead a captured Australian pilot who was sitting on a block of wood. He remembered the touchingly white knees of the blindfolded man, and the tall sword, raised flashingly in the tropical sun, that would swish down in less than a second, whereupon the head would fly through the air and the body, in those ridiculous short pants, would fall sideways. He had often wondered whether *he* would have taken that photograph, and he thought he would not. He shuddered.

'Doesn't *this* exist in time?' he asked.

De Goede shrugged his shoulders.

'Certainly it does. But what you see is something you assume to be pure, holy tradition. And that is how they like to sell it too. These gates open only once a year. Then the people are allowed just for once to walk on these garden paths that normally only the Emperor walks on. And Emperors there have been here, as you know, ever since the blurred, misty past. Twilight of the Emperors! They go back for centuries before Christ. I believe the present one is the one hundred and thirtieth. And a direct descendant, too. So you're linked to primeval times here, and that seems to be a happy thought to many people. All I see is a bunch of militaristic bullies who refuse to tolerate the slightest improvisation. This nation is sick with obedience. Don't you dare step out of line.'

Deliberately De Goede now took a step sideways, thus bending the imaginary rope out of true. Immediately one of the officers advanced with angry strides, to push him back into line.

'A thousand reproachful eyes now pierce my back,' De Goede said cheerfully, 'But I am a Flemish Giant, I can stand it.'

At that moment the immense gates opened.

'What happens now?' asked Arnold.

'Wait and see, and keep your holy visiting card at the ready.'

A slow-moving throng, they entered the imperial gardens, or rather, they were driven like a flock of sheep until they reached, in full view of the massive palace, a row of trestle tables on which all the men, apparently without exception, deposited their visiting cards.

'The Son of Heaven will be reading all these tonight,' said De Goede cheerily. The Japanese around them lingered for a while, gazing at the blind windows, but no one appeared, no man and no god, and with gentle pressure they were led away, to make room for the next group.

Almost mechanically Arnold Pessers spent a couple of films on the stately, melancholy splendour of the imperial flowers, but his thoughts were still on his friend's earlier words.

'I still don't quite understand what you mean,' he said, after his Leica, with soft sighs and clicks, had swallowed the purple and gold magnificence.

'What I mean by what?' asked De Goede.

'By space and time.'

'It's very simple. A manner of speaking. Most of the English and Americans who come here – not necessarily the business men, for they are undeceived very quickly indeed – but let us say the artistic types, have no real knowledge of Japan at all. They know it's different, but so are Vietnam and the Ivory Coast. Japan, if you will forgive the expression, is differently different. But how do you explain that to them? They don't speak the language and in most cases never will, they know a little, which is really nothing, about Japanese culture, but that doesn't bother them, they have something better than knowledge, they have an *idea* about Japan. And this idea always has to do with a certain form of asceticism or purity or whatever you like to call it. To put it briefly, it comes down to this, that they are convinced that the Japanese have managed to keep their heritage intact better than other people, as in some kind of pure, unadulterated culture.

Purity is the watchword. The *pure* beauty of calligraphy. The pure aesthetics of flower arranging, of eating, of daily life. The ugliness, the stupidity, the ruthless slavishness with which the Japanese copy our worst habits, the buying of mass products, the ridiculously aped decadence: they refuse to see it. The poetic types are the worst. They never stop talking about the samurai writing poetry at a time when the languages into which these poems are now being translated had not yet been invented. As soon as poets start talking of soldiers and commerce you'd better watch out. 'The samurai class stands by the cradle of the present day economic miracle in Japan', I read the other day. That was written by a compatriot of yours. Holy mother, they practically believe themselves to be fully-fledged Buddhists when they've read a twenty-page pamphlet, they write haikus in their Western hotel rooms, but forget to switch on the television, and they wander around the temple ghetto in Kyoto armed with a Polyglot Travel Guide without noticing the differences in style between the various periods. The disappointment always comes later, and then they make a complete about-turn. Then they never stop complaining, though without the punch of the true haiku: 'The Japanese are so inaccessible, you can't get through to them, they don't understand anything, they don't speak any languages, they just smile politely, they have no individuality, they sell out to the West, they don't deserve their country. And so on.'

'What do you think of Japan then?'

'I think that the Japan they are talking about, the Japan they *first* talked about, did once exist. Once upon a time. Before we forced it to join us. The madness of it. Wanting to drag by hook or by crook an island that lies like a shrimp stuck against the big belly of Asia, into the wake of our morbid progress. Commander Perry. Small events, evil consequences.'

'So there once did exist something like it?'

'Something like it, yes. Perhaps. Once upon a time. Long ago.'

'And nothing is left of it?'

'Enough. But you have to search for it. And it is not accessible, it never was. To Lafcadio Hearn, perhaps, then. Or to Sieboldt. But not to us, now. We are lazy and they have changed. Although . . .'

'So what do you think of Japan?'

De Goede stood still. For the first time, a shadow of doubt appeared on his usually impassive face.

'I understand nothing about Japan,' he said. 'I know a lot and I understand less and less. Last week they took a German colleague of mine away by Lufthansa, screaming in a straitjacket. Japanitis they call it. He spoke Japanese, had done his Ph.D. thesis on Bunraku, he had a Japanese wife, you name it. Ran his head against a wall, exit screaming.'

'East is East and West is West?'

'No, it isn't that,' De Goede said impatiently.

'I spent some time in Bangkok, and in Ulan Bator of all places. No problem. Lots of problems, but no problem. But this mad mixture . . . There's going to be a big Tokugawa exhibition in London soon, one enormous display of holy, untainted Japan, all of it pure culture. You won't find a hint of the incredibly bloodthirsty dictators which the Tokugawas also were. Only their art remains, just as with the Medici. Art can be used for anything, even for selling Toyotas.'

They paused by a group of oddly-clipped bushes. They look like animals without heads, thought Arnold Pessers. He did not take a photograph of them. It was as though these bushes were lying on the shorn lawn, as if they could not have roots. He looked at the deep, mournful purple of the maple trees beyond, and then at the people walking toward the exit in silence as if they had experienced something for which no words existed. Suddenly he noticed how much taller and coarser he and his friend looked. A Van der Weyden and a Jan Steen, De Goede had once remarked mockingly, and it was true: in some mysterious way their beloved ancestors had carried those inalienable features, via an infinite progression of matings and pregnancies, unaltered through the ages into this Japanese garden, and here they stood briefly, more in the role of descendants than anything else, as the solid, pale products of another race. They don't even see us, he thought. They don't want to see us. There was something strange about it, to feel at the same time so solid and yet so invisible, as if you would be able to fly despite your weight. It made him feel slightly dizzy and he decided not to think about it any more.

'And yet I am fond of them,' said De Goede, as if he too had taken stock. 'Do you know what I think is the oddest thing about them? All their greatest heroes are failures. In a country where people prefer to hide in a crowd and not to be noticed, the few madmen who go against the grain and fail hopelessly are the heroes. As long as they fail, as long as their end is cruel and desperate and their doom predictable. I have a book about it, *The Nobility of Failure*, you ought to read it.'

2

The Nobility of Failure, this title had impressed itself on Arnold Pessers with the force of a slogan, a formula you could mutter softly to yourself and which then acquired a mysterious power. He had remained silent for the rest of that afternoon, but now, so many years later, he recalled the quintessence of that conversation in its full intensity. He entered a fashionable espresso bar and sat down, in the purple neon light that can make the Japanese skin look such a deathly grey. The irritating exemplariness with which the people here were dressed oppressed him, as if he was having an evening out in Zwolle, but he did not want to go back yet to the apartment he had just come from. The woman he had left there must be asleep first, only then would he go back. He closed his eyes and saw the photograph he had not taken. '*Après l'amour*', it should have been called, he thought maliciously. They had slept together – for the last time in the room where they had slept so often before – two strangers inside a deathly silent cube, human beings, members of a strange animal species that could in no way have anything to do with the ceaseless traffic of the metropolis which, somewhere far below, sounded like a double bass continuously playing the same note. Love-making was, with them, usually a soundless event but, he could not think of any other word for it, always dangerous. He had never experienced this with anyone else, this sense of threat, this challenge of anger and warfare coupled with unintelligible professions of love and caresses disguised as bites. But it was exactly for that reason, he knew, that it was love – a love he would have liked to pour over her in buckets, covering that oriental, different, closed body under him, beside him, above him, as with a lasting light, and yet a love that at the same time had always retained a shadow of such terrible intensity that it frightened him, while this fear, in its turn, he did not know how, renewed his love, again and again, rousing and spurring his feelings and his tenderness. He then felt again, humiliatingly, that he was someone of a different race, someone belonging to a cheap, unenduring, banal kind of people that found it necessary to dispel the deeper emotions at all cost, by means of smoking, telling jokes and anecdotes, small talk, evasion.

So it was this evening. Thinking of the love affairs he had had in his life (the long life of a thirty-four year old photographer from Utrecht!) he knew these had never been more than a consuming of each other; two bodies intent on mutual enjoyment. True, this had sometimes been mingled with tenderness, or with that other ingredient which is, usually without justification, called love, but it had never been such a silent, almost vicious fight with the apparent aim of becoming the other, as far as that was possible. Was this nonsense? He was not sure, but it was what he had often thought: that he wanted to become her, and he felt, without either of them ever having said so, that something very similar was taking place in her, that she, mad though it might sound, was trying to take possession of his body, not in order to have him but to *be* him.

He would never be able to explain this to anyone. How can you tell someone, even your best friend, that you can know by the grip of a woman's hand that it is governed by a desire far exceeding any short-term possessiveness, that her hand had grabbed at his bones, his shoulders, his elbows, his knees, his loins, his head, wherever he was more bone than flesh, as if she knew that that was where his essence lay, that his soul resided in the hard, technical parts of his body rather than in the soft ones that would disappear so much sooner. He had learnt to keep such thoughts to himself.

3

He ordered a second espresso. One thing at any rate he was sure of, as he looked at the face of the girl who put his order in front of him, that it was not the Japanese in her that had attracted him in the first place. It was the Japanese *within* the Japanese, he could not express it any more clearly than that. To him, there would always remain something unreal in all those closed faces, but hers had by nature a double layer, not the plastic model of the westernized doll's head with the clipped eyelids that you saw everywhere around, but a mask underneath the mask, as if an older layer of the population, of the *people* were present inside her. Mongols, Ainus, Kirghiz, a magic, unknown tribe of nomads, a clan from the steppe that had settled within her, so that through her you were connected with long lost times, with something that no longer existed and that would never come back.

That was how she had looked at him, again this time, when he said he wanted to go out for a short walk. He always had to take care not to lose himself in her gaze for too long, otherwise he would lie sleeplessly beside her for hours. He had quickly opened the rice-paper sliding door and had stepped out. But before reaching the outer door he had turned round once more. She was already half-undressed and stood in the narrow opening, a white erotic statue, a scarcely-moving image against the bare interior of the Japanese room. His vision became double, that of a lover and a photographer. The lover knew he should not have looked back, because she would be lost to him as a result, the photographer on the other hand caught the entire image all the more eagerly in a frame: the rice-paper doors, the panels in the narrow wooden surrounds, painted with mountain landscapes in light grey shades, fine, washed brush-strokes hinting at rather than representing nature. Because the door had been slid aside, the landscape no longer matched. It seemed as if even the imagined world had become double, had shifted to one side, while in the centre a void had occurred behind which, in the middle of the room, she rose like a goddess of doom.

4

The first time he had seen her, five years ago, her face had received the name that he still muttered to himself now, whenever he thought of her. *Snowy mask*. He had come to Japan for an utterly banal purpose: to compile a travel brochure for a distinguished, though of course commercial, organization. But even if it had been a documentary about cement works or prisons, he would still have come. His world, and this was a fact to which he had resigned himself, was the world of brochures, of ephemera that no one would ever look at again; the decay, the sell-out, the morass. It wasn't actually so much a question of having resigned himself to it, he had taken a decision about it. He knew he wasn't good enough to be so independent that he could choose his own subjects, and even if anyone could, it was hardly possible to make a living that way. He had once baffled De Goede, when the subject cropped up, by showing him his favourite photograph.

'I always carry it with me,' he had said, timidly as if it were childish always to carry with you what was dearest to you, like a taxi driver keeping the picture of his wife and children on the dashboard. He had stuck the photograph to the inside of his camera case. It was his talisman, his amulet, but that was nobody's business. It was a page cut from *Zoom*. For a moment it had seemed as though De Goede would burst out laughing. His slightly rotund, soft white body wrapped in a too small kimono, had sunk lower into the chair, the hand with the signet ring had held the photograph away from him; he, Arnold, was not allowed to look at it now. But he knew it by heart, as if he had taken it a hundred times. It was a photograph from 1858 and there wasn't really anything in it. He had first seen it in the Notman

Photographic Archives, in the McCord Museum in Montreal. His attention had initially been drawn only to the shape, for while the two bottom corners were rectangular, as they should be, the two top corners curved rather oddly so that the whole photograph was shaped like a tunnel, a dark tunnel at that. 'The prairie on the bank of the Red River, Humphrey Lloyd Hime', it said, – and this was exactly what the picture showed, a grey, laden, *old-fashioned* plain in which prairie and water seemed to merge into each other without distinction. The horizon was a straight line; above it hung an equally desolate sky of a lighter grey, without any nuances. Two fields of grey, in fact, one darker, one lighter. And yet, when you looked longer, something like movement began to appear in those dead expanses of grey, a fraction of the light in the upper area had imparted itself to the darker area below, so that something of the light that had shone on that sombre river that day had been preserved; a few streaks, a few patches, a flicker, just as the light of the stars tries to speak of something that happened before there were people and would try to do so even if no people had ever come into existence, although in that case the question arose, why, or rather, for whose benefit?

In the foreground you finally saw, if you went on looking long enough, a faint, almost dirty line that was supposed to represent the bank, the beginning of the flat, no doubt muddy, land on which the ridiculous photographer must have stood with his tripod, drinking in light in order to record this sad, empty scene without people, trees or animals.

Albumen-silver from a glass negative. It moved him in a way that made him afraid to speak of it, for if he did he would have to say that you really ought to cry when you looked at it.

'*Mono no aware*,' De Goede had said.

'I beg your pardon?'

'"The pathos of things". That is a notion they have here, you'll hear it mentioned plenty of times. It means exactly what it says. It sounds like it too.'

'*Mono no aware*,' the photographer had repeated the words and had never forgotten them. They fitted the photograph exactly.

'What would you most have liked to photograph, if you didn't have to do all this rubbish?'

'Stones.'

De Goede had laughed, and what was worse, he had been unable to stop, until Arnold Pessers realized that this was meant to indicate a special kind of agreement. But that was all a long time ago.

5

Long ago, and at the same time a sort of yesterday. For that sort of time-recording no verb tenses exist. Memory flows this way and that between the perfect and the imperfect, just as the mind, left to itself, will often prefer chaos to chronology. It was with the passion of a convert, his Flemish friend had not been far wrong in that respect, that he had wanted to go to Japan, as if, so said De Goede, something could still be found there that had vanished almost everywhere else, except perhaps among the Touareg or in the hidden darkness of the Amazon region, but which at any rate could never be retrieved in the kind of society from which *he* had sprung and in which he, so it seemed, would have to remain for the rest of his life. The contradiction between these thoughts and the trite travel brochure, for which a lady in kimono against the background of Mount Fuji had been most particularly requested, he had brushed aside, along with the dismal sight of the drab warren of untidy streets, during the endless journey from the overcrowded airport to the hotel that looked exactly like all other hotels, anywhere in the world.

He had refused to feel disappointment and attributed the doubts he was so forcibly repressing to the wretched flight that had lasted for more than twenty hours. If you make up your mind to enjoy yourself you will usually do so. He had invested too much in this visit. He did not switch on the television in his hotel room but he admiringly examined the manner in which his kimono, put out for him on the bed, had been folded. He also gazed – as if this could banish the rest of the surroundings – at a reproduction of a calligraphic masterpiece, a black, furious trail of unintelligible but beautiful, exciting signs on snow-white paper. He ate in the Japanese restaurant at his hotel, where the food was exorbitantly priced, and delighted in the graceful movements and the high, gurgling voices of the waitresses. That there was something mechanical about these movements, because of the tiny, always identical, shuffling steps with which they went about their business, he did not want to see. He was in Japan. And *that* he was not going to have taken away from him.

6

The next day he had phoned De Goede, his friend at the embassy whom he had first met when making a documentary about Vietnamese refugees in Northern Thailand. De Goede had made himself available and together they had gone to a modelling agency where they worked their way through stacks of photographs of Japanese girls. Arnold Pessers had learnt how to see through the insipidness of such photographs – which were after all merely intended to sell a living person – but this time he was unable to find what he was looking for. The faces with the clipped eyelids had a slightly frantic look, as if they wanted at all cost to be different from what (but what was that?) they were.

'I want something more Japanese,' he had said finally, and he had noticed himself how ridiculous it sounded.

'But they are all Japanese girls.'

'Yes I know, I can see that. But I am looking for something more eh . . .'

'Younger? You want young girls?'

'No . . . no, you don't understand. I want something more . . . real.'

'To him they are all "real",' said De Goede. 'You won't get anywhere this way.'

He spoke a long sentence in Japanese, in which Arnold could distinguish only the word 'deska' or something like it, because it recurred again and again and seemed to indicate some sort of question. Each time the Japanese had replied to this 'deska' by something that sounded like 'Ach so', but the expression on his face had not changed once.

'As far as I can see he hasn't a clue,' said Arnold, displaying his friendliest smile.

'In this country you have to have patience, my friend,' was De Goede's reply.

The palaver went on endlessly. A hint of reluctance now appeared on the face of their oriental host.

'I want somebody who is not beautiful,' Arnold tried once more.

'O my God,' groaned De Goede, 'have you any fish that isn't fresh?'

A silence fell. The man looked at them impassively, but finally said in a not uncaring tone: 'Maybe in one hour I have girl you like.'

When after that one hour she entered, two things were immediately clear to Arnold Pessers. Firstly, that this was the woman he was looking for, and secondly, that her appearance aroused a tremendous tension in him.

Her name was Satoko, but he would call her that only on this first occasion. Her face, in an image that had been instantaneous, reminded him of a snowy owl he had once seen during a nocturnal drive through a northern mountain landscape. The bird had been visible from afar as a white, frightening object, and, groping for his camera, he had slowly come to a halt on the deserted road. The white mask, turned sideways on the body, had looked straight at him, burning from two round, yellow eyes, mysterious and hostile – but when he began, as cautiously as possible, to get out of the car, the owl had flown away, no, had risen up into the air. And now it was sitting before him, here in Tokyo, in the guise of a woman. She had a voice that matched her face, somewhere between high and low, a sound different from that of most other women. Her English was rudimentary but the silences between the hesitant words heightened the tension.

He told her he wanted to photograph her by Mount Fuji, preferably in different kimonos, and De Goede discussed with her the where and the how, 'for there are millions of possibilities, assuming the wretched mountain is visible at all. It has its head in the clouds half the time.'

It gave him a surprise to hear her speak in Japanese. The timbre of her voice deepened and sometimes, when De Goede said something that seemed to strike her as new or unusual, she lifted her mask slightly and said in a low tone, or half-questioningly, or at any rate on a falling note, something that sounded like 'mah' or 'meh', a diphthong that would become so dear to him. Finally, De Goede had reserved a 'real' *ryokan* for them, in Ukai-Toriyama.

'One or two rooms?'

'I don't know what is the custom here.'

'Usually it's not a question of how to start but how to stop.'

The next day it was radiant fall weather. She was at the hotel exactly on time.

'Today we can see Fuji.'

It was very early in the morning, but the traffic was already under way. They drove along a raised highway below which an unending landscape of drab human activity lay stretched out, but he paid no attention to it. Soon he would be outside the city, and see the real Japanese countryside. Something of Hokusei's one hundred views of the sacred mountain would become true, something of the graceful silence from a hundred haikus, of the inimitable, mystical emotion from Basho's journey to the Noeth. It was a good thing that De Goede was not there to read his thoughts.

'There is Fuji-san,' she said suddenly.

He looked but saw nothing. In front of them drove a gigantic tanker, its stench blowing through the open window.

'I don't see anything,' he said, and a thought flashed through him like a sudden stab of pain: *This woman frightens me*. Taking one hand off the steering wheel she pointed to a spot on the horizon that was as empty as the rest of the sky.

'You must look well.'

Suddenly he saw it. In the emptiness of the still smog-shrouded sky, there stood, faintly as almost nothing, the outline of the mountain, but in a way that it looked as though the sky was the solid element and the mountain an empty space cut out of it. There was something very ethereal, shadowy, non-existent about it.

'I cannot stop here,' she said apologetically.

He did not reply, and wondered how this day would pass. In the back of the car lay two kimonos, one light and one dark, folded with infinite care. The obis lay beside them, and the one on top, gold-coloured, caught the light of the sun and shone and burnt like fire. He tried to imagine what she would look like in these kimonos, and watched the strong, closed profile beside him. Thinking of the light, he asked how long it would be before they were there.

'There are many places.'

He decided to leave it all to God, and leant back in his seat. Everything he saw filled him with hilarity, not of the merry but of the ecstatic kind. Perhaps one should simply call it a feeling of happiness. He could see how ugly it all was, but the beauty of the ideograms and the script on billboards, road signs and trucks compensated for the larger ugliness, and anyway, they would soon be out of town. Only then would they be in Japan. Through the bends in the road the mountain could sometimes be glimpsed, sometimes not, and in the end it vanished altogether. A man motioned the traffic to leave the second lane but when they came closer Arnold saw it was a robot. The ominous feeling thus created, by the deadly regularity with which the mechanical hand executed its movements, he shrugged off. Later, much later, he would remember that robot as the first herald of a calamity that had something to do both with him and with Japan. Where the two converged, there lay his destiny. That was more or less how it had been.

That day he saw more views of Mount Fuji than Hokusei had ever drawn. Sometimes it looked as if it was all a deception, as if there were thousands of such mountains. They would suddenly reappear, behind a village, a wood, a field, always with that transparent snowy peak that sometimes seemed to float mysteriously in the sky, and then again to rest on solid matter. He could not gain a hold on it. From time to time he asked her to stop, ran up a hill, looked at the mountain through trees, or lying in the grass, or across the dark water of a lake in which it was reflected and therefore seemed twice as mysterious, but each time he tried, peering in his viewer, to imagine her in the picture, he knew it wasn't right. What he wanted, not so much for the brochure as for himself, was a place where the woman and the mountain would belong together in perfect counterpoise, would merge into each other, would hold each other in an unprovable but self-evident equilibrium. It should never be a woman by a mountain, a mountain with a woman in the foreground, or a woman with a mountain in the background. He himself, the photographer, would have to be present in it invisibly and the same time passionately, and he did not know how this was to be done. The mountain, though there was no clear way of proving it, was an erotic manifestation, its tall, pointed shape would add something to the eroticism of her face, as if it had become the symbol of a breast that had to exemplify, in the photograph, her breasts, confined under the kimono; a woman's breast turned towards the sun, away from the earth, representing, perhaps *being*, her invisible breasts, and thus floating through the sky, unapproachable, forbidding, and therefore arousing a longing that would become associated with her, though no one seeing the photograph would be able to say why.

7

After they had been driving for some time she said she knew of a place where she had been photographed before, in the same season of the year, for 'Swedish magazines'. The advantage of that place was that she could change her clothes there, and also that it was not far from the ryokan where they would be spending the night. Without waiting for his comment she stopped a few moments later at a tea-house by a bend in the road.

Later, when it was all over, he would ponder this question a great deal: when does such a thing as a great love begin? Perhaps it had already begun the first time he saw a portrait of a woman by Utamaro, perhaps during his long flight across the ocean, perhaps when he first saw her at the agency, or perhaps not. A great love, that inexpressible thing, poisoned by banality, probably started with the longing for one. And that longing he had had all his life. That had been the preparation for the moment he was standing here, listening to her voice in the tea-house, to the unintelligible ripple of question and answer in which permission was sought and granted, to change, in another room, from her European clothes into one of the kimonos she had brought with her.

She disappeared. He sat down by a window and looked out over a deep valley that, passing all kinds of capricious greenery, declined into a golf course and then sprang up again, both dark and airy, in the form of woodland, climbing up undulating, compelling slopes, in order to support the mountain that rode through the skies like a god in his chariot.

When she returned he realized just how much he was in love. It was a feeling he remembered from his school days, it raged through his body, it carried within it every possibility of pleasure and grief. The kimono was a rusty, burning colour, a stain of living decay kept in check by the chrysanthemum-golden constraint of the obi. She went out onto the terrace where an imitation temple gate stood waiting for all the world's amateur photographers.

'This very Japanese.'

The white peak of Mount Fuji hung above her head like the crown of the Snow Queen, the mass of the mountain itself draped her shoulders and flower over the paltry, so very Japanese, little gate. He went up to her to measure the light on her face, which had received a rosy glow from the sun.

'Yes, very Japanese,' he said.

So this was the equilibrium. Mountain, woman, gate.

She was a perfect model. Again and again she knew, by means of minute changes of pose and expression, how to devise different pictures for him. He had a phrase for it: she eats the light, and this was possible only because she knew exactly where the light was, her light. She worked with the light, she stole the light, she sculpted herself in ever different poses so that an eagerness grew in him which, when they finally stopped, made him feel dizzy. He let himself sink down onto the cold grass against one of the pillars of the gate and gazed at the mountain.

'Okay?' she asked.

'Yes. Very good.'

'I change dress?'

'Yes.'

She vanished. Tiny steps of her white feet. A shuffle almost. The silk of the kimono made the sound of a large bird flying low overhead.

The evening sky rose from the valley and drifted in veils across the road.

'Where do we go now?'

'Ukai-Toriyama.'

Why had he not remembered it? Ukai-Toriyama. He savored the sounds, pronounced them softly. This would always remain extraordinary: to sit beside a stranger in a car, on the way to a place you had never heard of before. Ukai-Toriyama. The strands of mist danced in the light of the car.

He closed his eyes.

'Here it is,' she said softly.

Whether he had been asleep for a long time or not, he did not know, only that he had dreamt that he was still in the aeroplane, high above the ocean, on the way to her.

8

They drove into an avenue flanked by tall torches mounted on poles, burning against the still pale-coloured evening sky. When he got out of the car he heard the sound of a water wheel and the isolated, monotone notes of a string instrument.

'What is that?'

'What you mean?'

'This sound. Ting, ting?'

'Oh. This is samisen.'

Samisen, a very light word.

Two servants in black took the suitcase. The

kimonos she wanted to carry herself. Something restrained him from entering the low building inside which all contours were blurred by the faint shine of a lamp. It was still not altogether dark, he wanted to walk for a while.

'I will come later.'

She looked at him but said nothing. I suppose it is un-Japanese, he thought as he walked away. Randomly he turned into a path that led past the outhouses of the inn. In the kitchen he saw cooks and girls in blue aprons. They could not see him. The path wound through low hills, to his left he heard the sound of a fast-flowing stream. He had a feeling as if his soul, which he must have lost somewhere above the ocean, was slowly joining him again. Somewhere in a bend of the path there stood a kind of altar on which several Buddhas were seated. They wore faded red sashes and sat there, detached from everything, against a background of leafless fruit trees behind which a sudden conifer-covered round hill loomed up. Now I have arrived, he thought. Now I have truly arrived. Just as in the water a lighter and a deeper tone could be heard, so a second, more distant hill became visible in the light-coloured gap between the dark conifers. He walked on. These Buddhas could never change their expression, the seasons that would cause the leaves of these fruit trees to brighten, fade and drop again, had no influence on their faces, they themselves were the seasons. In front of them there were flowers of a furious purple, on the ground lay some thrown-away orange fruit he did not recognize. He bent down, picked one up, pushed the hard skin aside with his thumb and ate from the sweet orange flesh. Then he turned to the purple flowers again. The leaves were long and narrow but the flowers themselves had a crumpled look, drops like quicksilver adhered to the green sepals. There was a curious oneness in everything, the sound of the water, the darkness that slowly fell upon the world, making the mist intenser, more sombre in colour; it all seemed to be one thing. And then there was the sound of the crickets, even now, in October, and that was what they cried, October, October.

He walked toward the sound of the water. From a bare bush between black bamboo stems there hung a single, blackened leaf, not by a stalk but by the broken, floating thread of a spider's web. It was as if nature, the otherness, that which surrounded him, wanted to penetrate him, take possession of him. He shivered and returned to the ryokan. A servant showed him to his cabin and called something.

'Hai!'

The servant motioned him to take off his shoes and slid the door open. She stood as if posing for a photograph, and photographers know best what that means. She wanted to be seen in her chosen stage setting, and then preserved.

Arnold Pessers could never look at a photograph without thinking of this. He found nothing more fascinating than photographs of strangers, taken by strangers, preferably so long ago that all the people concerned were sure to be dead. And sometimes he was absolutely certain that he himself was taking such a photograph, a picture that an anonymous passer-by would one day, somewhere, find on a stall or in a store. What would that stranger see? He would see what Arnold Pessers, the then nameless photographer, saw now, stained by the passage of time – but that could always be cleaned off – a Japanese woman in a kimono, standing in a low, sober room, to her left a kakemono with one single flower painted on it. Other than a low table there was no furniture in the room.

Her kimono was grey with red and gold flames, her piled-up hair gleamed in the same yellowish light that also shone on her intent face. She stood motionless, frozen, stage-managed. With his miniature camera and flash he took her in ektachrome, rapidly and so rhythmically that the soft hissing clicks of the shutter sounded like a metronome.

Something passed, not seconds, but photographic time, a time in which time was swallowed up and preserved.

When he had finished, he said 'You are very beautiful.' The limitation of this phrase pleased him. Only when people understood few words, could they understand everything. This was very comforting, language always spoilt so much among co-linguists, because, he reflected, as soon as words were uttered, lics were spoken.

The door opened. A girl in a simple blue kimono entered on her knees, pushing a small wicker basket containing hot cloths ahead of her across the floor. A second girl brought a dish of raw fish and two rough earthenware saké pitchers, rather like miniature Greek amphorae with only one handle, of the sort that are laid on their sides in the fire. Satoko had sat down with much rustling of her kimono and poured out for him, the snowy mask bending forward, the black gleam of her hair toward him.

'Raw carp. Fish from river. From Ukai.'

Raw carp, starlings, quail, a fish called ayu, tofu, quail's eggs stuck on wooden pins, river trout impaled on spikes in a last undulating motion, everything was pushed into the room, accompanied by the muttering of soft, murmured formulas, the servitude of the girls was soundlessly commuted into her own, she grilled, poured, smiled – but whether or not this signified anything he did not know, for she scarcely spoke. So they sat crouched on their zabutons like a Japanese couple after twenty years of married life together. From time to time they looked at each other, indicating with their eyes or with foolish little gestures that this or that was delicious. Whenever his bowl was empty she refilled it for him. Each of her movements was of a flowing gracefulness, there was nothing left to wish, to desire, to ask. From outside there still came very softly the sound of the samisen, weaving its golden thread through the silence and the almost inaudible purr of the water wheel. After the green, slightly bitter tea, she very briefly and very lightly put her hand on his knee.

'We shall walk garden?'

The torches cast pools of dark, theatrical light on the glistening wet tiles of the garden path. He felt surrounded by sounds, but each of these sounds was small and in itself insignificant, the brook, a waterfall, the slowly-churning wheel, the shuffling of her high wooden sandals on the ground, the fronts of her kimono brushing against each other, the sighing of the wind in the bizarre nocturnal shrubs. She had taken his hand, it was as if she was performing a dance with him, a dance in the labyrinth of that garden that could not exist anywhere except in a forever vanished age. Behind the rice-paper windows he saw the shadows of other people, from some of the small houses with pointed thatched roofs there came the sounds of laughter and music. It existed, he thought, and at the same time it did not exist. He did not belong to it, he was here with her and yet he had nothing to do with it. It would cast him out in the same way that a body rejects a transplanted heart. He tried to push aside the word 'dream', but it kept floating to the surface and what he felt was again that crazy mixture of sadness and happiness, so intense that he could hardly bear it. And all the time, persistently, he remained the professional photographer, he went on looking, taking pictures with his eyes; a water butt, a dwarf tree, a chrysanthemum like a weapon, a rustling shadowy crop of reeds.

When they returned to their own little house, the light was muted, and at the place where the table had stood there now lay, on the gently springy rush mats, a bed with a light quilt turned back at one corner.

That night there began the only real love story of his life. When, later, he once tried to talk about it with friends, he discovered that you can speak of such things only in the most basic terms and that these are at the same time the terms that most arouse ridicule and incredulity. But it could not be helped. It was a passion that would burn him down to his roots and through which all that came before and after would fade, because this time it was love first and foremost and only secondly a story. Pleasure, they say, is forgotten as easily as pain, and perhaps this is true. But the *event* was unforgettable. What he had felt he would have to experience every time afresh in order to know it again, but what he had seen had remained – the shadow dance of torches and bamboo stems outside against the paper screens, the absolute, relentless intensity of everything she did, the mingling of sweat and tears on the white gleaming face which had remained a mask, then and forever after, the tension and the bursting into a hundred fragments of her body, which would haunt his memory always, rotating sequences of close-ups, of her matt, translucent skin, the shape of her breasts, of her open, outstretched arms catching him somewhere in the air and pulling him down, and especially the gesture of a hand held desperately in front of her face in order to hide the highest ecstasy while the other fluttered helplessly through the air and then fell like a bird that will never rise again.

Later, when she slept in a forlornness such as he had never seen in anyone, he lay looking at her and wondered what was to happen to him. *Three* masks she was now wearing, one on top of the other, the Asiatic, that of her own impenetrability, and the third, equally unrevealing veil of sleep. Long ago, on the dresser in his parents' house, there had stood a sculpture of a girl's head. It was, his father had told him, the death mask of an unknown girl who had been drowned in the river Seine. No one knew her name. It was someone who had existed and who now existed no longer, no one would ever know who she had been. That sculpture had frightened him, and fear was what he felt now. He would like to take her photograph but he dared not. The light of the flickering torches outside fanned across her face as if wishing to waken her to life again. Gently he covered her round, gleaming shoulders and turned away from her. Something had begun that would obsess him for the rest of his life.

9

For the rest of his life. Five years ago he had first thought that, and it had never changed. He stared abstractedly at the girl before him who was telling him that the espresso bar was closing. 'We close, we close.' He paid and got up. The five years between that first night and this moment when he was walking through the Ginza like a desolate stranger, he had spent mostly outside Japan, but it seemed like one long curved leap of time in which everything had had to do with her.

The morning after that first night they had taken photographs in the neighbourhood, and toward noon they had gone back to the inn at Ukai-Toriyama. He had noticed a strange, sweetish fragrance and asked her what it was.

'It is Mokusei.'

Mokusei is one of the few Japanese plants that smell, he learnt later, and that was what he had called her from then on. Now she had three names, one secret, only known to him as Snowy Mask, her own, Satoko, which he never used, and Mokusei. By that name he wrote to her, it was a name that existed only for them. How easily, he now thought, could the history of those five years be summed up. During that first visit they had stayed together day and night. But she had refused to come to Europe with him.

'My parents, when I go, they die.'

He had never met those parents. They lived in Osaka, and she did not want to take him there. At their parting she had cried and he himself had sat in the plane like a bundle of misery. Back in the Netherlands he felt restive, roamed about like a homeless animal, pestered his friends with stories about her, which they found at first amusing and later boring. His relations with women acquired something mechanical, something abstracted, as if it was not really permissible to have anything to do with them, and of course in a way this was so. Finally only those of his women friends remained who were either excited by his total lack of interest or who found it convenient for other reasons which, out of self-preservation, he preferred not to know about. Often, during such encounters, he imagined what she might be doing now, he calculated what time it must be where she was, and it was probably his concealed rage at such thoughts that made the relationship so fascinating for his partner of the moment. After one such meeting he had torn everything from the wall, in seething despair, including her portraits, because he felt she should no longer be a witness to what he regarded as betrayal. On the bare wall above his desk he had hung a Hokusai reproduction. It was the severed head of a woman. The eyes were closed, two lonely dark lines, but the mouth, of which the lower lip was redder than the other, was open. A lizard was sitting on the chin of the head which lay among reeds, amid the loose waves of its own hair. To the right of the face there glimmered a patch of blood, very lightly painted; this red and the green of the lizard were the only living colours, all else was brown, the single, light brush strokes of the reeds had been drawn across the still face. Sometimes it looked as though it were laughing, or trying to say something. He thought it ought not really to hang there, but it wasn't frightening, in spite of the bee which hung almost directly above the face and which, when he was alone and looked for long enough, he could hear buzzing. One of his woman friends had said it was morbid, and he agreed that this was so.

But there was no help for it. His phone bill soared to astronomic heights and the conversations left a burning emptiness that could only be filled by more conversations. Sometimes she was away from home for days, but he had learnt not to ask questions about that. Her voice was a mask as well, it seemed. He knew nothing about her life. Her parents, her work, that was all. Once he had asked De Goede if he could not find out a bit more about her, but he had said, no I can't, my friend, that is not what I am for, and he had felt ashamed. She did not want to come to him, De Goede's efforts in that direction, which he had undertaken without objection, had been of no avail. After a time, his friend had been transferred to Singapore, and so the last person they both knew had gone.

During his leave in Brussels they had dined together and De Goede had advised him to break it off. 'Believe me, I have seen it before, you must end it or you'll go to pieces yourself.' Arnold had got drunk and asked why his friend always wore such ridiculous pocket handkerchiefs, and De Goede had replied 'for fear of death', and then they had got drunk together and misbehaved themselves in a Japanese restaurant, and that was not the only time that Arnold Pessers got drunk in a Japanese restaurant.

But whenever he obtained a commission that enabled him to travel to Japan, she was at the airport, and they went back to her Tokyo apartment as if he had never been away. He always tried to stay as long as possible, on one occasion for almost six months. That his debts in the Netherlands mounted and his bank would no longer give him credit, worried him more than he admitted to himself, but because of the distance it seemed as if these things could not be quite real, and anyway, his whole existence had become unreal, as if all this were not happening to him but to a stranger, a hired actor who, when he looked in the mirror, bore a curious resemblance to him, Arnold Pessers. Sometimes she left for a few days. Then he stayed alone in her apartment and went into the city in the evenings and sat among the other expatriate Europeans in the Pub Cardinal in Roppongi or hung around in discos where Japanese disguised as negroes in raffia shorts served the drinks, or where electric miniature trains whirred all along the walls, until he had reached the right pitch of insanity. This was definitely the 'other' Japan, a spiritual slum of failed imitations, a country he hated the way you hate a rival. All those things that he loved her for, the remoteness, the enigma, the inaccessibility, here seemed to have been converted into their opposites, showing him a different mask, of mechanized vulgarity, that threatened him and would eventually drive him away. But he never spoke of this to her.

10

That was how it had been until now, until this strange, silent moment, when he was walking here and heard his own footsteps on the emptying pavement. But this evening everything had become different. The sword, he reflected, that he had so long expected, had struck, flashing, deadly.

She had taken him out to dinner at the Imperial Hotel, and in that sumptuous setting she had told him that this was the last time he would see her, because she was going to be married. It had sounded like a lesson learnt by rote. 'I want to be near parents. I don't want to make trouble. I want to make house and have children.' The fact that she had added I love you, with that slight hesitation in the I that had always attracted him so, was no help. He had told her for the hundredth time that he too wanted to be married and have children, but then her face closed again, showing that it was impossible.

'It cannot be.'

He had come to the end of his thoughts, to the end of his walk, and entered the apartment. She slept her dead, drowned sleep, but this time he would take her photograph. From his suitcase, which was already packed because they were going to Ukai-Toriyama the next day, also for the last time, he took his tripod and an ultra-fast film. He would have to use a flash. He re-arranged the sheet a little. If it was too smooth she would look really dead in the photograph. That was superstition of course – probably because that 'dead' look was part of her sleep, but in the photograph he wanted to be able to see by the colour and the details surrounding her that she was really *asleep*. Someone who is asleep is at the same time nearby and far away, from you and from himself, powerless and yet powerful, precisely because of that distance. Only at the sixth or seventh flash did she wake up.

'I don't like. When I sleep it is not me.'

'Yes, it is you. I know.'

'No. When I sleep I have no eyes. I am not blind person.'

She turned over. He lay down beside her, but he did not fall asleep until it was almost morning. He felt the warmth of that body of which he knew every tiny detail and which he had seen in an ecstasy he would never again – he was certain of this – be able or want to arouse in anyone. And at the same time he realized that he knew nothing about her and never would. He would have liked to break her open in order to know her secret or at least to find out what were her feelings for him, if she had any. He fell into his sleep as if into a fathomless hole in which he would have preferred to remain. But farewells had to be said first.

11

That last day became a replica of the first. The time between these two days, with all those longings, letters, declarations, nights of love, all those dramatic phone-calls across the grey steppes of Siberia, evaporated and were annihilated in the one moment that, with the eternal mountain still floating in the distance, he took the picture he had already taken five years earlier. Even in the prints, later, you could not see that the woman standing there had grown five years older, still less the sacred mountain. The same woman, the same photograph, the same fall day, the same inn, the same smell of Mokusei. Life as memory: the samisen, the water wheel, the torches, the servant preceding them. This time again, as before, he wanted to go out for a walk. With a movement of her hand she checked him. She pulled him down beside her on the tatami, undressed him, undressed herself. Never before had she been the one to take the initiative. They lay naked on the mat beside the low table. This, he thought, is war rather than anything else. Fury mingled with her love, a fury corresponding to his own. Biting, devouring, penetrating the other, absorbing, robbing, with all the hopeless frenzy of people who want to become one another, want to be one but cannot, who are always again forced to part, to leave each other, gathering empty rooms behind themselves in which gestures and words, the maimed language of never finished phrases, will dissolve among the impassive objects waiting for the next guests or not waiting but merely existing. He felt like someone who has to swim an immense distance and has come half-way, too far to go back and too far to go on. When she finally let go, turned over, away from him, burying her face in the fine rushes of the tatami, when her whole body had once again become a closed, unassailable fortress, an object he had no longer anything to do with, he stood up, dressed and went outside. It was a shade darker than the first time. He walked past the Buddhas. Here, too, nothing had changed; with difficulty they had counted out one second in those five years. A dwarfish old woman, bent low under a heavy burden of brushwood, came toward him like a bad omen. Branches, fire, ashes. The brook rippled, and who should he have been, to hear a sound different from that of the first time? He walked further than on that other occasion. On the wet path he saw the furry skin of a nut, trampled, crushed. All objects now seemed to acquire a meaning, the discolorations in the last green that could still be discerned, the fungi on a tree; black, damp patches on the bark of a birch, everything was trying to say something. From time to time he paused, registering the movement of the swift water past a gleaming black boulder. It was as if he was counting something, but he did not know what it might be. Even if he could have done so, he would not now have wished to take any photographs: this, for once, would *not* be preserved, this was for him, and only for him. He took a path leading upward, into the darkness, stepping on some thick smooth bamboo canes that had been placed across the stream as a footbridge, listened to the gurgling and swallowing of the water. What vanished feet had worn away this path, had made it into nature? Under the surface of the water the ground itself seemed to be aflow. Somewhere there lay a pile of logs, a firm dark shape as if they had grown together. A hundred years ago a woodcutter had been here, had stacked them ready for the next day but had never come back. Mokusei. He heard himself saying her name aloud, and stood still. So this was fear, what he was now feeling. Something irreparable was happening to him. He turned round. Out of the direction from which he had come, strands of mists advanced toward him, shredded, floating shapes intent on attacking him, ready to encircle him, envelop him, hold him imprisoned by that stack of wood, a hundred years, a thousand years, for ever.

When, panting and scratched and still pursued by the mists, he arrived, running and stumbling, at the inn, her car was no longer there. The faces of the servants expressed nothing. He went to their room and slid back the door. On the table there was only one rice bowl. For the second time that evening he heard himself saying her name while she was not there. Mokusei. He took off his shoes, went in and crouched by the table. Now he had to enter upon the sadness that would never leave him all his life, even if he lived for a long time. It would fade, like everything else, but he would never escape the feeling that it was he himself that was fading away.

THE PHOTOGRAPH

Rachel Billington

Lillian lay in bed dying. Or so everybody assumed. Even her stepdaughters allowed themselves to hope. She herself believed she was the reincarnation of her husband's previous now dead wife and that she would live on to look after his motherless children. It might have been thought that these children were old enough to look after themselves; they were three girls, Elspeth, Daphne and Flavia, ranging in age from twenty-five to thirty-five, all were married or in Daphne's case had been married and none of them had lived at home for years. Lillian was not deterred. She felt herself at the centre of a protective web.

Hesketh Weld, her husband, thought she was dying because she had suffered two severe heart attacks in two months, and was bedridden. She would not let him leave her side except to do the continual errands she required. 'I must have iced water, Hesketh, not this horrid lukewarm stuff.' She had become very petulant. Hesketh who was ten years older than her sixty and not very well himself, struggled valiantly up and down the steep stairs of their converted oast-house. She deserved no less as a woman and his wife.

Lillian had brought the oast house for them when they married eight years ago. She was French and rich, having inherited her previous husband's property. She thought the oast-house charming. With reluctance Hesketh had sold his 14th century stone farmhouse. The girls, of course, had been furious. All their memories of their mother were linked with this house. Pansy Weld had been as beautiful as her name and had died of cancer three years before her husband remarried. Her daughters had worshipped her. So had Hesketh. He had enjoyed forty years of happy marriage. The children believed Lillian had caught him while he was sad and defenceless. Daphne refused to see her father for a year after his marriage. She considered Lillian inexpressibly vulgar and petty. The most important event in her life was the arrival of the silk camiknickers she had always worn from Paris. And it was true Lillian seemed to consider her new life an opportunity for sacrifices in others to ensure her comfort. She even stopped Hesketh doing his two days' work in the City which he so enjoyed because she felt deserted – although she said it was to protect his health.

Daphne, the middle daughter and the one who had only been momentarily married, was the cleverest and the most beautiful of the sisters. She was also much the most loved by Hesketh who thought her like his dead wife. In fact all the girls gave a similar impression of great height (they measured round the six foot mark), with enormous luminous blue eyes and floating chestnut hair. When they were together it was like a meeting of the Valkyrie or certainly the members of another race.

They always did meet in their father's house at Christmas. It was the least they could do for him. It was never a smooth occasion but this year promised to be particularly difficult – with Lillian dying so commandingly upstairs. They did not know where her scheming had led her.

Lillian had always been particularly keen to take Daphne under her wing. Quite simply this was because Daphne liked her least and of all his daughters Hesketh loved her most. For some months, even years, she had desperately wanted a large close-up photograph of her so that she could put it in the living room to keep company with herself and Hesketh. Daphne had even offered her a few but they had been rejected as not clear enough or not quite like. Then a few weeks before Christmas when she was already more or less bedridden after her first heart attack, Lillian discovered just what she wanted.

She told Daphne about it herself over the phone. She had found it in the Fortnum and Mason Christmas catalogue. A quite lovely photograph of Daphne – well, not actually of Daphne since it was a model showing off Ciro Pearls but just exactly like her. Everyone in the village thought it a marvellous likeness. Lillian's triumph was not open to reason. Dissatisfied with merely cutting out the photograph she sent it off to an expensive Bond Street photographer to be copied even larger and then, despite her second heart attack, arranged for it to be mounted in an antique silver frame. It would be her Christmas present to Hesketh.

This extraordinary behaviour even further convinced the family that she was about to die. Already she was out of her mind.

Lillian however lay upstairs planning and scheming and exhausting Hesketh with her constant demands. A week before Christmas she asked him to post a letter to Fortnum and Mason. In it, though she did not tell him, she had asked for details of the Ciro Pearl model, her name, age, statistics – and if possible a photograph in profile. Fortnum and Mason replied with the name and telephone number of the model agency who had supplied her. Lillian's excitement increased.

Elspeth, Daphne and Flavia arrived with two husbands called John and Peter on Christmas Eve. The oast-house which was filled with the nooks and crannies so beloved by Lillian but with no large room, seemed suddenly very crowded. The main celebration, it was decided, would take place in Lillian's bedroom on Christmas Day over lunch when she usually felt her best.

The room which Lillian had been living in almost continuously for several months was warm and fetid, smelling of a mixture of medicines and scent. The girls thought that the rich odour of turkey and Christmas pudding could only improve matters. They were all very shocked at the wan appearance of their father and said bitterly when out of his hearing that they hoped she died before she killed him.

Christmas morning was a particularly grey dismal day. Drizzle ran down the leaded window panes. None had the heart to go out for air although they all felt horridly trapped inside. Only Lillian seemed happy; she sparkled, she glowed, her cheeks flushed hectically; she refused to take a rest and insisted on taking champagne. She had not looked so well for a long time. The girls struggled dismally over the lunch, hating as always Lillian's presence, hating particularly the need to sympathise over her health and hoping out of it all to salvage some happiness for their father.

It was he who opened the door to the girl. She stood on the doorstep, very small, very pale, very wet.

'Prue Scully. I'm looking for Mrs Weld', she said nervously.

'She's not well', replied Hesketh bleakly.

'She hired me from 12.30 pm.'

'I see.' He turned and led her in, past the girls busy in the kitchen, and up the stairs. He presumed she was some sort of nurse.

Lillian lifted her head from the pillow and flung wide her arms when she saw her. 'Oh, my dear!'

Hesketh retreated out of the room. He was glad to see

Lillian occupied and too tired and numb to question her flamboyant welcome.

The girl stepped into the fuggy room. No one had asked her to take off her soaking mackintosh and it began to steam. Realising this was not going to be a job like other jobs, she spoke in a mixture of anxiety and defiance.

'They did explain at the agency it's triple rate on Christmas Day?'

'Sit down. Sit down, my dear. I assure you, we are not thinking about money here. Or at least in no way that can possibly harm you. On the contrary it might do you a lot of good.' Lillian giggled rather hysterically. She waved her champagne glass at a chair and since the girl still remained standing, cried imperiously, 'Sit down! Sit down!' In fact, she wanted to forget the girl's height which was a foot or so less than Daphne's.

'Daphne,' she cried. 'My own!'

'Prue Scully,' said the girl.

'Of course. Of course.' Lillian became ingratiating. And then as Prue made a move forward as if to shake hands, continued irritably, 'No. No. I've especially put that chair there for you.' Really Lillian didn't mind that Prue's wan little features were not the slightest bit like Hesketh's daughters – with her new plan it was hardly relevant. Nevertheless she did not want to see her too clearly.

Downstairs the girls, their faces flushed, were lifting the turkey from the aga. The Christmas pudding was already turned out and standing in the warming oven; the smell from the brandy butter on the table filled their nostrils.

'One more Christmas lunch just about launched.' Elspeth tipped out the sprouts.

'Thank God.' Daphne spoke for them all. Calling

their husbands and father to follow, they formed a procession of meat and plates and vegetables up the stairs.

Hesketh said from the bottom, 'There's a girl up there. A nurse.' But no one took much notice. Peter and John clinked their champagne bottles together and bellowed a few lines of 'O Come All Ye Faithful' to cheer up their wives.

Prue huddled in the dim light of Lillian's bedroom and watched it fill with noisy giants and steaming dishes. She was not noticed at first. Till Lillian announced in a horribly shrill voice, 'I want you to meet someone very important to me.'

The husbands stopped singing abruptly and the girls put down their burdens. They followed the direction of Lillian's quivering finger. (How they hated that finger which bore one of their mother's pretty Victorian rings!)

'Now Lillian,' said Hesketh wearily.

'There she is!' cried Lillian triumphantly as if doubting their ability to see.

'Do you mind if I take my mac off?' whispered Prue as the giant figures took a step nearer. 'It's absolutely soaking. And it'll ruin this nice chair.'

One of the husbands who was least able to stomach drama began to sharpen the carving knife. It was his special duty to carve the turkey.

'White or brown meat?' he asked Lillian as if she were not fixed in an attitude of frenzy.

'More champagne?' said the other husband nervously.

'She'll get more than that.' Lillian's shrillness had become menacing.

Daphne suddenly realised that this poor little girl was the model from Fortnum and Mason's catalogue who was supposed to look so like her. She wanted to laugh at the absurdity of the situation but was stopped by Lillian's livid face. Really she looked on the verge of another stroke. A guilty frisson of hope passed over her at the thought.

The husbands began to hand round food. They distributed a stack of little tables and paper napkins. Elspeth, the oldest daughter, said she had forgotten the bread sauce and went down to get it. During all this inconsequential activity Lillian stayed silent but her glaring excited expressions did not change. It was as if she was merely waiting. Eventually everyone was settled and even Prue had accepted a plate handed graciously to her by Flavia. Otherwise she was ignored, rather like a bomb too delicate to be touched. Everyone felt threatened by her unassuming little presence.

Then Lillian threw down her knife and heaved herself on top of her pillows. She looked like a spiteful Buddha, Daphne thought; she glanced at her father and the strained pallor of his face banished any pleasure in the idea.

'I know you've never liked me. None of you. I know you've hated me. I know what dreadful things you girls say about me. When I love you so much. I know you think you're beautiful. Clever. Superior. When I only want to look after you. But I think you're like the three witches. Great gaunt women with your mean hard looks and horrid works. When I always wanted children of my own. You think you hate me. I know. But I hate you more. Oh, yes. I hate you, so much more that I'm never ever going to let you go. You and your father.'

The girls looked at their father. Now he must see what a dreadful woman he had married. But Hesketh didn't seem to have heard anything. He wore a dazed, blank but unshocked expression and even ate slowly at his food. He had stopped listening to his wife months ago. All he wanted was peace. There was no help for him from himself.

'You see I've got my own Daphne now. My own daughter now. Better than the three of you put together. She'll let me look after her.' Now Lillian was waving her arms about and bouncing ludicrously on her pillows. Her greyish hair which she wore curly and rather too long, snaked and jumped around her face which changed from pale to red in terrifying psychedelia. The girls stared, fascinated. The husbands ate their turkey stolidly. The reminded themselves Christmas was only once a year and drank some more champagne.

Lillian screamed: 'I'm adopting her. Your father and I are adopting her. My daughter. My own daughter. Someone to love me. Someone for me to love. And when I die she'll still be herc. You'll still have her. Your father will still have her to look after. And she'll remember me. She'll be part of me!'

The three girls sat in an unmoving row as Lillian's voice rose to unnatural heights. Though they did not show any reaction, Lillian's plan seemed to them a macabre possibility. They looked at Prue's uncomprehending face and thought that she could never resist Lillian, even without the lure of an inheritance. They must not let it happen. She couldn't have arranged adoption papers yet. Daphne turned back to watch Lillian and was struck again by the idea that she looked near to another heart attack.

Daphne leapt to her feet. She towered about her stepmother. She shouted down at her with fierce blue eyes, 'Oh, no, you don't. Oh, no, no. No, Lillian. You can't have me!'

Daphne knew how her stepmother hated to be contradicted; how it enflamed her ego; how it touched some extra spring of energy.

'Ah! Ah!' Lillian began to shriek incoherently.

'Oh, no, no, no!' continued the great dark figure of Daphne looming over the bed. Usually she was slow, so majestically slow. It made this ferocious energy all the more terrifying.

'Ah! Ah! Ah!'

'Daphne. You'll kill her!' gasped Elspeth.

'No. You cannot. Jamais, Jamais, Jamais!' Her stamping foot shook the bed.

'Aiiieeeeeh!' A ghastly inhuman whistle rose out of Lillian's gaping mouth and pierced all their ears till they tingled horribly. Prue clapped her hands over her head.

Lillian tumbled off her pillows and fell onto her face like a baby. Her hair coiled over her head and landed in her turkey and sprouts. One arm fell off the edge of the bed and swung like a bell clapper against the side.

Daphne's eye was caught by her stepmother's Christmas presents stacked ready under her bedside table. On the top was a square package garlanded with gold ribbon and addressed to her father.

'Just look at her lovely present for Father.' Her voice had slowed to its usual deliberation. 'What a frightful tragedy!'

HANS PFEIFER

Giles Gordon

In this tale there is neither hero nor heroine. Nor are there villains. It is, if anything, more about disengagement than engagement. There is no attempt to explain that which is irresolvable.

If you will, now read on.

Brand is a village in the Vorarlberg, Austria. It is dominated by the Schesaplana mountain range. From away up in the mountains it is possible to look down on or across into both Switzerland and Liechtenstein.

It is picturesque and unspoilt, in spite of – from December to March – being taken over in the winter, snowy months by invading skiers, holidaymakers. They mostly come on package tours, and stay a week.

There are eight drag-lifts and chair-lifts, and a number of well-managed, hospitable hotels including the Colrosa, close to the village church and about eight minutes' walk from the centre of the village and the main chair-lift, the Niggenkopfbahn; Sporthotel Beck, with a tiny indoor heated swimming pool, table tennis and a sauna for both sexes at once (if the idea appeals) and in which the middle-aged Austrian women invariably appear unclothed so that any tan they achieve is even all over; the Valschena has spectacular views of the mountains; and the Hämmerle, which provides packed lunches for guests on full board if, as most do, they want to stay up in the mountains all day: early meals and cots are available on request as well.

In the summer, Brand is visited by walkers, most of

whom wear lederhosen and Tyrolean hats, and carry alpenstock, or at least sticks.

Thus the village, in the latter years of the twentieth century, is principally concerned with holidaymakers, holiday-making. There is farming, and looking after land and animals, but, depressingly, it seems a subordinate activity.

So small is the village that there are no pavements, not even on the main – almost only – street or path through the centre of Brand. During the winter months, after falls of snow, snowplough lorries will appear, apparently from nowhere, out of the air rather than a garage, and push their way up and down the street and into paths off the main thoroughfare and shift the detritus from the sky into heaps, to left and to right.

The snow will lie first white, or whitish, then become grey, then the piles will lower in height and become brown slush and eventually cease to exist.

Every morning, including Sunday, Frau Pfeifer sends her son Hans to do the shopping. The Pfeifers live in a large enough solid, wooden house two or three minutes' walk above the church. The church is towards the head of the valley which cradles Brand. Hans leaves home to go shopping at the same time each day, and returns at the same time. He leaves at 10.55 am and arrives back just before twelve.

By the time he sets out the village is wellnigh deserted. Life in the morning and afternoon of the skiing months, from morning sun to the onset of dark, the fading away of the light, is up in the mountain. Until 10.00 am the chair-lifts carry the skiers upwards and upwards until it seems they will merge with the elements.

The skiers set out in the mornings from their warm

hotels. Wearing great, heavy ski boots they move – like a phalanx, an army – through the village, converging on the lifts. The young men feel vastly pleased with themselves in their combative gear. Many of them wear ludicrous outmoded moustaches, – recalling *Viva Zapata* or *The Three Musketeers* – others absurd wisps of beard. Perhaps they can manage to grow no more or don't have the energy – the atmosphere in the mountains is heady, exhausting – to shave them off or don't feel it worth buying a razor to demolish such trivial growth.

There is a machismo sexuality in the ski clothes, not least in the outfits worn by young women. It seems to turn them into latter-day Amazons. As men and women walk slowly, solemnly through the village in their great weighted boots, carrying over their shoulders their skis and holding their sticks, it is like some outlandishly costumed production of *King Lear* played on an infinite stage.

They reach the chair-lifts, don their skis, slither and slip towards the lifts, and two by two sit in the chairs and begin the voyage upwards. Up, up the mountains they go. They pass the occasional flag in red, white and red horizontal stripes, the Austrian flag, fluttering or drooping. The chair-lifts, ascending and descending, are utterly unhistrionic. It is eerie that, even when occupied, carrying people up or down, they appear to be lifeless and only make a sound when their wires connect with the upright pylons supporting their weight. The whirr of the machinery is, somehow, muzzled by the weight of the snow below, lost amidst the whiteness.

Up, up, the skiers are carried. Soon there are more at the top, or high up, than on the ground, waiting to ascend. People speak little to each other. They do not wish to communicate, make conversation – on the lifts or when skiing – or express anxiety. A broken leg is a broken leg, so there is little point in worrying about it.

Down below, in the street, two or three yellow buses ply backwards and forwards, carrying those with chair-lift passes from the base of one lift, the Niggenkopf-bahn, to another, the Palüdbahn. They also take the villagers from, perhaps, their homes to the shops. Hans Pfeifer always walks though, that is what he does, walks to the shops to do the shopping he does. He is a slight, gangling figure, whose limbs seem sometimes not to be co-ordinated. He wears odd, floppy wellingtons to keep out the snow, grey trousers and a blue anorak.

'Time for the shopping, Hans,' Frau Pfeifer says each morning; and Hans gathers up his bag and sets off down the path, down the hill. The shopping bag dangles from his arm, his wrist.

By then few people are left in the village except for the elderly and children, and those having to make a living, running a hotel or a guest house. When they venture out they look like Babushkas, befurred and huddled and hunched. A little boy, with a wondrously carved wooden hobby horse prancing between his legs, walks home from school. Why he has been released at this hour he isn't going to divulge to all and sundry.

A few visitors trail the streets, and each other. To some, a little adultery is, perhaps, more enjoyable on a skiing holiday, a kiss and a cuddle or two, than swishing around on the pistes. Oh the silly innocence, the guilty silliness of human kind.

The sun comes and goes, coming and going. Great sudden heat is contrasted with sudden, shivering cold, a huddling into furs, sweaters, thickest of socks.

Half-way up is the Hubertus-Haus, the expansive open air café by the Palüdbahn lift. Bare tables are scrubbed and scrubbed. Better to eat, surely, steaming hot goulash soup and roughly textured bread and sausages galore, drink frothy and bubbling beer than the insanity of gorging Eskimo ice cream. The ice cream recalls the terrible comment of Ophelia's brother, that he would shed no more tears as of water she had had enough.

From there, hundreds of Christmas trees are seen. Not that they look like that, not as in Trafalgar Square or the individual homestead, even an Austrian hotel. They are an essential, inevitable part of the natural habitat, grown from the rolling, jagged mountains. To grow and grow over many years; to ask no questions and have nothing asked of them. Trunks, pines by the million, dark green against the amazing, outrageous blue, the white landscape, hillscape, the physical presence of the living trees, the trees alive.

Down below, Hans is on his way to the shops. He will get there, visit the three or four shops he visits. There aren't many more than that, not many more. The Spar supermarket (now there's a shock) provides most essentials but he doesn't only shop there.

Some things are so silly. Occasionally someone, usually a girl or young woman (when does the one become the other, especially when sheathed from head to foot in ski clothes?) throws a snowball. She gathers the snow, throws the snowball, watches the projectile in the air, then splat, it hits someone or something, powder and break. The poor broken snow.

The chair-lifts continue, continue to carry the skiers up and sometimes down. Without apparent reason, they stop for a minute or so, no sound in their stopping, no sound in their beginning again. People sit there in silence, not moving, as the chairs stop.

When they reach the top, the skiers ski off the chair-lift, off the slope. In their flashy outfits, goggles, sticks, skis and heavy boots like weighted lead they melt into the unmelting snow, disappear like ghosts of the mountain tops. There is a paradox between the cumbersomeness, the weight of the weighed-down skiers, of being downed to earth and how, taking flight on their skis, they are liberated. They soar and fly with skis attached to their boots, they skim and swoosh and carve and dive and are become unearthly.

Giant icicles hang down from any projecting roof, or high wooden surface. Hanging there, the iced water, against the weight of the snow, they look like hand-swords of the gods. Mortals cannot cope with the weight or the sliding slither of the vast icicle weapons. They hang silently, ominously, time ticking away, not seeming to drip just to gain length, solidity.

Below, the snow ploughs move up and down the village, parting the white. The yellow buses ply up and down, fewer of them than earlier, when more in demand.

Hans visits the shops.

Every time the sun shines strongly, a little snow melts. Its resistance is weakened.

Clouds rush about, fanned by the wind, warmed by the sun, obscuring the mountain tops. Soft puffy clouds become the swirl of the majestic heights. Sharp and angular, like gods' elbows, the summits are etched, engraved into the sky. There is a thrilling intensity in the hard artefact against the ethereal, giving almost the illusion of it all being three-dimensional. On top of the highest mountain top is a cross, a Christian cross; whether constructed there by man, built, the upright beam nailed into the horizontal or a freak of nature, of foliage or of the light, is not to be affirmed. The cross seems to be there, is therefore there.

Hans has completed his shopping. He starts to walk up the village street, not thinking of home yet but starting to return. If he knew what would happen.

Up above, having an early lunch at the Hubertus-Haus, sun tan lotion is applied to bared, supple limbs. Skiers with mirror glasses shift their faces. The mirror glass reflects no one, neither the wearer nor the worn, the skier contemplating the skied. In bed, in the hotel rooms below, one idiot, otherwise naked, keeps on his mirror glasses while making love to a girl he's met two nights before. On the mountain, the mirror glass reflects the sun. The wearer of the glasses becomes an acolyte of the sun and harbours an illusion of magnetic power.

You can hear birds, the very occasional bird, like life renewed after the Flood. Then the skish and swoosh of skis, the spray of driven, savaged snow, the running of gleaming water, the blades of the skis, as if polished for the occasion.

Skis at Hubertus-Haus are stuck upright in the snow, stabbed there, standing up; yet another male symbol within the female. If left there for long enough, would they grow, burst into rockets, contemplate higher achievement? Who says the inanimate hasn't in it to become the animate?

Then snow falls. The landscape stills to a silence, a peace, is utterly quiet, as the snow – heavy or soft but either way consistent, even in its falling – drops. Does a snowflake contemplate its past, its history from years ago as it draws within feet of the ground (look, it is falling; shush, do not waken it; the dream of a snowflake falling through infinity, then kissing the ground, touching, kissing, melting), cease to have individual, unique identity; become but part of the snowscape? And it shines with its own light, sparkles like granite – as hard as that – when the sun deigns to catch it, turn it, flicker it.

Christmas trees, against the angles of mountain and snow on the hard edge of the silhouette, stand upright not as if from effort, from growth but from some lively game.

The shopping bag still dangles from Hans' wrist, his arm, although as he returns home it is not empty.

He is nearly there, getting there.

Then it happens.

At seven minutes to twelve the clock strikes, the church clock.

Oh Hans, Hans!

He swings round on his upward hill walk, having passed the church. He swings round to look at the church clock.

Hans is aged thirty-three.

There is nothing else really he is able to do but he helps his mother every day by going shopping. He doesn't buy much but his mother doesn't ask him to buy much. She gives him each day a list she has written out and he hands it, does Hans, to the shopkeepers. There isn't much money in the Pfeifer home. Luxuries are unknown, and items other families might consider essentials are regarded as rarities, luxuries if you like.

He lives in the village, always has done. And now he is thirty-three. He lives here but he is apart from Brand, has never been a part of it, as baby or child or man. What, come to think of it, is a man, a child, a baby? Somehow, the repetitiveness of the process, that it takes (roughly) three generations to achieve a century, a century to achieve three generations, suggests we do not know, that there is a lack of confidence in the process of birth, of regeneration.

Hans thinks: If the first man was so good, why make

a second? But there's an answer to that: If the first man was so good, God-good, let's make a second in his image, to prove it wasn't a fluke. And of course it was. The second man didn't live up to the first, he was a disappointment to his father. Not, ironically, that he was that much worse than his father, if at all, but that he wasn't, in his father's eyes, that much better. Adam, the father, the first, expected much more of Cain, the first son, than he expected of himself. And so on, each father of his son, ad infinitum; and there is Hans, with his dangling bag, treading the main street of Brand.

The yellow buses continue. Children return from school. A little adultery is achieved. Up above, at the Hubertus-Haus, a huge hunk of icicle drops into the snow and no one notices as it falls. Someone, in the café, turns on a transistor. There is a warble of, perhaps, American pop music, burbling out, stifled by the apathy of the limb-tired skiers.

Seven minutes to twelve, the clock strikes. Hans Pfeifer is more than bewildered, bemused. He is appalled, his universe – the skull and the village, the valley and the mountains – has disintegrated. His world is ending. He has to be home by twelve. No one has ever said so (why should they have done? What else is there for him to do? But he didn't know, understand that) but he knows he has to be home by twelve. And today he won't be, can't be, it is twelve already, no, the clock has struck. He is in the street still, on the snowy slow hill. He has, simply, failed. Or rather: the clock, the church, the world has failed him and he, Hans Pfeifer, can't live with that. The natural, necessary order has become at a stroke, the stroke of twelve, unnatural, unnecessary disorder.

He cannot go home. There is no point, even if his mother welcomes him at the door, by the log fire.

There is no home for him to go to. Disorder is rampant, chaos has prevailed.

Up in the mountains, the skiers ski on, glinting and swooshing, curving and diving. Oh what a jolly, hedonistic, head-in-the-air time they are having. Their mouths wide open in fresh laughter, perfect teeth a-shining, a-sparkling in the sun. How they laugh when they fall, even fall badly, and bruise their bums and buttocks and thighs to a black ripeness. Imagine that, through their expensive ski-fashion outfits.

Hans hadn't ever understood, didn't understand the alien, visiting seven-day world that gave the village life, breathed it into if not, exactly, existence but an ability to continue for another seven days, the packaged skiing week, beginning on Saturday evening when the coaches brought the white newcomers from Zurich to the following Saturday morning when the same coaches took the browned visitors away again. Nor did he understand the world of the village, why it existed only thanks to the skiers, yet tried, insisted on leading a life of its own, where the community, the inbreeding of families, thc opening of hotels if not lederhosen was adequate for a way of life, a rhythm – not just adequate but *was* the way of life. And the church was the centre of that, and the church spire incorporated the clock, the clock the outward symbol.

He squinted back at the clock, standing there crazed on the hill, shattered. He squinted back as if his eyes saw nothing outside his head, were able to comprehend nothing in the physical world but were turned in on themselves, a searchlight fragmented to the brain, an attempt to interpret what was within.

His brain embraced, encompassed his whole being, as if his life could be comprehended only in the terror of those seconds as the church clock struck. Not just the clock, not only, he didn't, Hans didn't, see it only that way, he saw it as the church and the sacrament, the life-giving sacrament that was lord of rule, that organised reality, discipline, sanity.

The clock struck early.

Now, if a clock strikes, rings out early – or late, that would be as bad – at a time which isn't on the clock face, how can life continue in orderly fashion?

Then, he moved.

You may think that he was standing there for ages, almost ever but only a minute or two, in literal time.

It wasn't that the chair-lift operators were negligent, not at all. They took some pride in the care they took. There weren't accidents on their lifts. Why, there wasn't even a resident doctor in the village.

Hans was too quick for them. Besides, they knew him, had seen him around for years, even chatted to him not that they ever got far, and thus didn't really notice, pay any attention, because he was always, ever there, if not where he was now (he had never been there) but in, around the village. Of course he wasn't wearing skis and he clutched his bag, it dangled from his arm, his wrist.

It was as if he flew to the chair-lift, the Palüdbahn lift, and somehow he was on it, sitting – no ticket of course – huddled in a corner, his back to the seat's back, as if welded in, made with the chair.

'Hey, Hans? What are you doing? Where are you going?' Caustus, the chair-lift operator called out, having left his ticket office, the base.

Hans turned his face to look at Caustus, whose name he did not know, but said nothing. The distance between them was increasing, growing. The chair, the lift continued upwards. One or two people were coming down but nothing special, nothing out of the ordinary.

Back in the village, it didn't occur to his mother to wonder where Hans was as it wasn't yet twelve.

In the church, Father Rosanna the priest assumed that no one would turn up for mass. He took a cursory look but no one was there. Which is not, not necessarily, to say anything about other mornings, any other morning, weekday or Sunday. But today nobody came to mass.

'Hans, you've no ticket,' called out Caustus.

Again, no response.

Hans was away, up he went. He soared, swung up on the lift, the chair.

Caustus, still standing there, gestured back to Edinger, behind the glass, to stop the mechanism.

Hans hung there in his seat, high up from the ground.

There was nothing anyone could do. He was way up, aspiring to the angular, rocky heights. Just because they were covered in snow didn't mean they were soft.

Below him, half-buried and battered by winter after winter, by wind and by other weather, were a number of stunted stone and wooden huts, shelters for animals. Hans looked down on them. No one would come to them until Spring, and by then it would be too late.

Then he laughed, laughed at Caustus and Edinger and everyone else, not that anyone knew. His laugh was of both triumph and despair, of having escaped – so he thought in a flash but the flash went, was lost and forgotten – from the inevitability of a routine-blasted life.

Caustus was back in the ticket office. A few sentences were exchanged between him and Edinger.

Caustus nodded; Edinger started the lift up.

Caustus picked up the telephone receiver and spoke to Haidacher at the top, where the lift ended. He explained what had happened and Haidacher said he'd look out for Hans when he got there, in eleven or ten minutes.

And that, really, is all. Hans Pfeifer never arrived at the top, nor did he return to the bottom. No one saw him leave the chair-lift but there were, at that time of day, few people on it.

Thereafter, his mother did her own shopping. But then she always had.

NEAR FORELANDERS KOP

Clare Colvin

After the heat of the day a light breeze comes in the evening. The two women watch the sky fading as they sit over their drinks on the stoep. Birds swoop overhead in their communal excitement before dusk falls, and from the servants' compound they can hear the sound of a penny whistle, thin and piping with a broken beat.

'I'm so glad you're here, because I never drink alone now,' says Diana. 'I haven't had a gin and tonic for two months.'

She has blonde hair, and skin that is tanned and dried to tautness by the sun. She has a lovely face, always had, but you can see the map of lines beginning to form. Jenny is paler because she spends her working days in an office. She is attractive, with short dark hair, and you would not particularly notice her as she walks past in the street. The two women have an ease together that comes from a friendship made during their years at college, and from the fact that they loved the same man and that Jenny realised it was natural to lose him to Diana. You would expect a man like Jan to choose someone as golden and beautiful as himself. They looked so right, both tall and fair, with that smile that enveloped you with warmth. Diana married Jan and left Cape Town to live on the Eastern Transvaal farm that spread over several thousand acres of bleached grassland and scrub, where he bred cattle and horses.

The insistent sound of cicadas is swelled by the croaking of bullfrogs from the river.

'I wouldn't live anywhere you couldn't hear the

cicadas,' says Diana. 'They mean warmth and sun. I missed them so much when I went to England.'

A man is walking from the servants' compound towards the stables. He wears a dark, battered hat and his shirt flaps loosely on his thin body. He has a slightly lopsided look as he walks slowly, in a dreamlike way. His right arm is in proportion with the rest of the body, but the left hangs uselessly, a wasted limb without muscle.

'There goes Stamford,' says Jenny. She waits for Diana to speak. Diana watches Stamford until he is no longer in view.

'He's taking an interest in the horses again, that's something,' she says. 'You know, after it happened he spent three months lying on his bed, not speaking. Irene had to feed him with a spoon. If she hadn't looked after him he might have died – I think he wanted to.'

Jenny is never sure how much Diana wants to say. She takes a sip of her drink and waits.

'Poor Stamford,' says Diana. 'Jan helped him so much. He was just a cripple living off his sister, and Jan gave him his work and made him feel useful. He said he was one of the most intelligent boys, but the others treated him as if he was simple. Sometimes in the morning I see him standing over there looking towards the stoep as if he is waiting for Jan to come out and holler for him to saddle up. It's as if he can't get used to not seeing him. There are times when I can almost see him, too. He had so much presence, that man.'

It had been early morning. The slanting sun's rays shone into the stoep and Jan, as he stood there, looked more golden than ever.

'Stamford, saddle up!' he shouted. There was no

sign of Stamford, but next moment he appeared from the servants' compound and loped towards the stables.

'Saddle me Trooper and Sunny Boy for yourself. Ready in ten minutes.'

Diana sat over her cup of coffee in the dining room, making a list of provisions. The room was darkened by the shade from the stoep and the blackwood table and carved chairs. They had lived there for ten years but little had changed from the days of Jan's parents. After his father had died, his mother had returned to Cape Town, where she had come from, as if that was her true home and she had only been transplanted to the veld for all those years. Diana was sure that she herself would never leave the farm, whatever happened.

The whitewashed building contained their entire married life. Everything that was important to her had happened here. Jan and she together in the night, their skins damp with sweat from the heat and their love. Being delivered of Piet, named after Jan's father, then of Winston – her family name, not after Churchill, she had to keep telling people. Jan holding her hand at the second delivery, which was less easy than they expected, the strength flowing from him until he was exhausted as well. Occasional parties when friends came to stay with bottles of Cape wine, and they would get pleasantly drunk as a relief from the harsh and uncompromising land. When would it ever be green again? she asked during the summer. Her friends from the Cape were a relief, too, from their few neighbours, Boer-bred and dourly foreboding of Jan's management of the farm. They did not like his easygoing ways with the boys, the softer you were the more they took advantage, they said. Jan's father had inherited the farm from his father, but they were of English stock. Jan's mother had at one time been a member of the Progressive

Party, and Jan said that apartheid was an unjust system and you should do what you could privately to ease it.

It was why he took an interest in Stamford, who seemed at the bottom of the heap, looked down on by his black brothers as well. It was his sister, Irene the cook, who first asked Jan to find work for him. Never disagree with the cook if you value your stomach, said Jan. If the rest of him is in working order, it doesn't matter about the arm. One leg is just a bit lame, but he is very willing, said Irene. Stamford began to ride out with him when they exercised the horses. Jan liked the feeling of quiet intelligence that came from him, the way he could use him as a listener for his thoughts, and the way Stamford responded without trying to make his own mark. Stamford, for his part, seemed to grow in confidence. He looked at you when he spoke and his eyes were bright, not dull and hopeless as they had been.

'Do you really need to ride out today? Some of this shopping isn't going to wait much longer,' said Diana.

'I'm not happy about the area near Forelanders Kop. Old Van Rooyen told me he had seen vultures and we have a hundred head there. Tomorrow I'll go into town, I promise you.'

Jan sat on the stoep cleaning his rifle, then went to the medicine cupboard and took out the snake-bite kit, a tin box with vials of serum and a hypodermic. No one went anywhere without it. The high veld was the land of deadly snakes. Lastly there was the bushknife, which he strapped to his belt. Stamford brought the horses round to the house, and Jan put the serums into one of the saddlebags, together with the bottled water and packed food.

'I'll be back before nightfall, don't you worry,' he said. Diana watched them ride away, the tall blond man on the rangy bay, the slight, lopsided boy on the speckled pony. Later, she remembered thinking, What an unlikely pair, and then, some women never meet the man they should marry. I did, straightaway.

The riders jogged along the dusty red track through the white grass. Most of the land could be reached by jeep, but this area to the east had outcrops of rock and streams that ran over boulders towards Kaophoek Dam. At seven o'clock the air was still fresh, but in the space of two hours it would reach the oven heat that lay on the land for the rest of the day until the breeze in the evening. Trooper was shaking his head vigorously as he trotted along and exhaling his breath in snorts.

'Has this horse got ticks or something?' said Jan.

'No, baas. He say he not been ridden for too long,' said Stamford. Sunny Boy was jogging quietly, his neck stretched forward in a resigned way. He took no notice of anything. You could stand on your head in the saddle and he would not react.

Trooper's ears pricked forward towards a rustling in the scrub, and Jan kicked his flanks, anticipating a shy.

'Don't you start spooking with me, boy. Hasn't Joshua taken him out?'

'Joshua have pain in belly. He not well for too many days.'

'Joshua's been at the beer again, he's got a pain in the head.'

They jogged on for a while. A few impala half a mile ahead scattered in a flurry of white tails bounding over the grass. A go-away bird took off from a thorn tree, cawing warnings of men with guns.

'I never heard why you are called Stamford,' said Jan. 'Where did you get that name?'

'It was Miz Mary at the mission school. She say she come from Stamford town in England, so she baptise me Stamford.'

'Stamford, eh? Lucky for you she didn't come from Wigan.'

Stamford grinned. 'Too right, baas.'

They rode in silence, until Jan said, 'I'm going into Willemsdorp tomorrow. You want to come?'

'No, baas. You remember last time?'

Everyone remembered last time, about a year ago. Stamford and Joshua had gone into Willemsdorp on a Sunday to see some relations of Joshua's. Two police officers had arrested them at ten o'clock in the morning before they had even got to the township. They saw the way Stamford walked, accused him of being drunk, demanded his papers and then relieved him of his pay packet. He arrived back at the farm almost too frightened to say what had happened. Jan got into the pickup and drove into town to see the commandant. He shouted at him. 'I give that money to my boys for work, not to go into the pockets of your scumbag men.'

The commandant shrugged and prevaricated, but Jan stood immovably there, towering over them, the force of his anger not to be denied. Eventually a face-saving compromise was reached. The policeman who had taken the paypacket claimed that it was an on-the-spot fine, and there were so many cases of drunkenness that it was not worth bringing them to court.

'The boy is crippled, not drunk. Either you give the money back now, or you charge him and take him to court.'

The commandant agreed it was not worth going to court, and perhaps the officer had got the wrong impression. The money was returned and the commandant said, as a further face-saver, 'I knew your father well, so I can trust his son.'

Jan looked at him in contempt and left the station without another word, but the story got around and was enjoyed by both the white farmers and the Africans.

'You called them scumbags,' laughed Stamford delightedly.

'And so they are – a bunch of bullying scumbags.'

The track had become a single file trail skirting around boulders. By midday they stopped to eat in the shade of a thorn tree, having checked the area around for snakes or scorpions. The silence over the land was profound, and even the cicadas seemed to have given up, exhausted. Only the occasional swish of a horse's tail, and the jingle of their loosened bits as they chomped the feed in their nosebags. Jan lay back on the ground, and covered his eyes with his hat. Stamford sat a couple of yards away, watching him and watching out for any sign of danger. These were the only times when their roles were reversed, when he felt he was protecting the man who protected him. In repose Jan's face, usually restless and alert, had a calm innocence about it. The rifle lay by his side, within a split second's grasp, but the arm beside it was relaxed and at ease. Stamford looked at him sleeping and felt a loving warmth for the man he was keeping from harm.

Jan sat up with a jerk, as he always did after resting in the open, and crammed his hat back on his head.

'No time to waste. Let's get on, Stamford. Stop those horses eating. Where's the water bottle?'

They rode past the remains of two shacks. There were signs nearby of cultivation at one time. The earth was not quite overgrown by veld grass and there was a scattering of mealies growing wild through the weeds. There had been African squatters a few years ago, but they had been tracked down and transported to a designated black area. Jan had protested, not only because he thought it wrong to force anyone to leave the land, but he paid them to keep an eye on the area for him. The authorities conceded that the men might stay if they were employed by Jan, but their families must go. One man stayed for a few months, but the loneliness got to him, and he left for the rows of little concrete houses that had been built for them on arid ground a couple of hundred miles away.

'That's what you get with apartheid – you cut off your nose to spite your face,' said Jan. 'When will they unravel it all? This is the most beautiful country in the world and the unhappiest.'

Stamford looked at him sympathetically, but said nothing. Politics was the most dangerous subject of all. One of Joshua's brothers had gone to a meeting in Barberton and been locked up and beaten by the police, and he had heard of guerrillas from Mozambique killing Africans who were working for whites. All politics, from whichever side, was to do with violence and killing, that much he knew.

They reached Forelanders Kop by early afternoon. The cattle were grazing peacefully, but there were vultures circling overhead, as Van Rooyen, who owned the land adjoining Jan's, had said. They rode among the cattle checking heads, and whether any of them were sick. A couple were missing but they found them to the west of Forelanders Kop. Then they rode round to the east of the hill. In a stone gulley a hundred yards away lay the carcass of a wildebeest. Three feeding vultures flapped into the air as they approached.

Jan dismounted and took a closer look, examining marks on the ground for some time, for signs of men or large animals. Then he returned to Stamford and the horses, looking unworried.

'Not as bad as I thought. The wildebeest got into difficulties in the gulley and some hyenas finished her off.

We'll get a boy out here to keep an eye on the cattle until we move them closer to home. I can't keep trekking out here every time Van Rooyen sees a vulture.'

'Him afraid for his cattle,' said Stamford.

'Quite right. He's not used a rifle for years. Wouldn't know how to. Wants me to do the dirty work.'

From Forelanders Kop, the lake below glinted in the sun. Jan looked longingly at it. His shirt was soaked with sweat and his feet were swollen. Foam from Trooper's neck laced his arms, and his head throbbed in the heat that rebounded from the rocks. He knew better than to swim in the lake where you could not see what moved under the water, but there was a tributary stream leading to it that splashed white and clear over the boulders.

'We can take the horses to drink at the stream and then we'll get back home,' he said. They led the horses over the pebbles that spread outwards from the stream, stranded in the drought after the rainy season until next year's rain brought another crop of pebbles spilling over the bank. Stamford splashed water on his face, but he did not take off his shirt as he was conscious of his arm. Jan had already taken off his shirt and plunged it into the water so that it could dry on his back. Looking downstream he saw the corrugations of the water ease into a clear, deeper pool. He flung a stone to see if anything was lurking there, but the ripples spread outwards without disturbance.

'You look after the horses, I'm going to have a swim,' he said. He stripped off his breeches and boots and laid the rifle on top of them, then plunged into the pool. Stamford led the horses some distance away. He felt an unaccountable sadness suddenly at that careless, golden dive, a twinge of discontent, Why could I not be like that? The thought was disturbing and he retreated further with the horses, and kept his back to the river so that he would not think like that any more.

The cold water embraced Jan, and the sparkling points of light on the surface dazzled his eyes. He plunged his head under to ease the throbbing. It was still and cool, insulated from the harsh glare outside. He swam a few strokes, then surfaced again and struck out for the bank. It was steeper than he expected, and he scrambled up, falling on one knee. As he got up, he felt the soreness from a graze. Clumsy of me, he thought, as he limped momentarily on the stones, for he was usually perfectly athletic. He looked round to see where Stamford had gone, and for those few seconds did not watch the ground as he walked.

There are moments when you feel a constriction on your heart as if an icy hand has grasped it. It comes when you drive too fast and you are suddenly into a bend. Skiers get it when they misjudge a leap and climbers as a foothold below them crumbles. Jan had felt it before, and knew as his foot stepped on something alive and moving and muscular that it was the hand of death.

There was no time to think anything else. A flurry and hiss, and then reared up and staring straight into his eyes, the snake. He saw the hood flared round its head and knew it was a cobra. The snake lunged forward and there was a blow to his chest and a burning sting. His first thought was, 'My gun', and he moved, without being aware of having moved, ten yards to where the rifle lay on his clothes. He turned and shot twice at the snake. The second shot severed its tail. It slithered towards him, bleeding, angry and in pain, and tried to attack him again, but it could not rear up to make its strike and flailed on the ground. Jan's next shot took its head off.

He had lived too long with the possibility to panic.

He knew that, with a bite to the chest, there was no remedy in tourniquets and bloodletting. It would have to be the serum. But where had Stamford got to? He finally saw him near the Kop, about 200 yards away with the horses. That two hundred yards stretched like mile after mile before him. Any movement hastened the flow of the poison to the heart, and would put him past the help of the serum before he got to it.

The boy had heard the shots and was looking around him, then, seeing Jan, began to run towards him.

'Get the snake-bite kit, Stamford. I've been bitten by a cobra.'

Stamford stared in horror, then ran back to the horses. With his one good hand, he undid the saddle-bag and took out the box. Jan sat on a rock, trying to breathe normally, calming his mind, thinking, The serum always works. He could see from Stamford's wide eyes and open mouth that he was in a state of panic, and called, 'I've killed the snake. Keep calm, just bring me the syringe. Don't rush, walk quietly towards me.'

Stamford walked more slowly, but his legs were trembling and his balance unsteady. One foot slipped off a stone, and the ankle bent, but he managed to remain upright. Then, as the other foot touched another stone which moved, he lurched forward. His good arm clutched the box and the withered arm uselessly tried to keep balance. As he hit the ground on his shoulder, the box flew from his grasp, and the vials fell out, the glass shattering on the stones. The serum spilled, in a dark stain, on to the sun-heated pebbles and almost immediately began to vaporise. For a long time the two men stared at each other, then Jan said quietly, 'Oh God . . .' and a moment later, 'Don't worry, Stamford, it's not your fault.' But Stamford had seen the message in his eyes before the reassurance of his voice, and his eyes had said, as clearly as if he had shouted it, *You stupid, bloody kaffir*.

The cobra's bite can take as little as ten minutes to kill. Jan was strong and took an hour. Stamford tried to suck the poison from the wound, but after a while Jan said, 'It's no good, Stamford, it's got to me. Help me to dress before I die.' Stamford supported him to the shade of the hill, and sat with Jan's head on his lap, wiping the sweat from his face and trying to still the spasms by singing, the way he heard his sister sing her baby asleep. Then, at the end, he closed the eyes, out of respect for the dead, and to take away the memory of the moment when Jan had looked at him like the policeman in Willemsdorp.

The evening is darkening to night and the birds have stopped their flurry of swooping to roost in the trees. Diana traces a pattern on the condensation on her glass intently as she talks.

'I was out here on the stoep when they brought him in. It was early next morning, and they buried him as soon as they could dig the grave. For a long time afterwards, I felt as if I had been torn in two, as if part of me was missing. I went back to the Cape for a while to stay with my parents, and I saw Jan's mother. She looked as if all the life had gone from her. Then I realised that I must go on living, and that Jan wanted our sons to have the farm, and now his uncle helps to manage it. One or two of the boys left. Joshua got very sullen and took off one day without warning. At times I wonder whether it is right to go on . . .'

She is silent for a while, staring absently into the night. From the stables a dark, limping figure emerges and drifts slowly back to the servants' compound.

'Stamford,' says Diana. 'He depresses me. It's two years ago now and he still goes around with that blank, hangdog look. We told him he wasn't to blame, for Christ's sake. If anyone was at fault, it was Jan. He should never have strayed so far from the horses, he shouldn't have gone swimming. To be completely defenceless like that . . .'

'Stamford must have been very fond of Jan,' says Jenny.

'Perhaps,' says Diana, 'and perhaps he feels guilty because if he had both arms it need not have happened. But there . . .' she bites the rind from the slice of lemon, in the way she does when she finishes her drink, 'You never really know what goes on in their minds, do you?'

A TRANSLATOR'S FICTION

Zulfikar Ghose

North of Lima, on the coast of Peru – such was my experience during the five days that I had occasion to spend in that region – there is a sparkling clarity on winter afternoons that, as with the addition of water to certain liquors, begins to turn milky just before sunset: one imagines it is only the exhaustion of all the brilliance that had prevailed during the day and one looks at the empurpled western horizon in expectation of witnessing the sun's spectacular sinking, but the purple has already vanished, the fog has come in, and one realizes that phantom shadows have begun to waver over the land, and it is only a matter of minutes, while the sun has still not actually set, that darkness quite overwhelms the land. The following day, the risen sun does not dissipate the darkness, and just when one begins to despair of ever seeing again that glorious perspective of the Andes that, tourist guide in hand, one had seen from the south-eastern corner of Plaza de la Constitución, looking east down Paseo Colón with its splendid rows of cypresses, suddenly, around eleven in the morning, it is as if the lights are brightly turned on to illuminate the stage for the first act, full of optimism and gaiety, of a drama destined to end four acts later in a tragedy on a darkened stage.

The theatrical image is the somewhat fanciful figure employed by my host Señor Próspero Aguilar from the terrace of whose house overlooking the Pacific I first saw the fog rising so dramatically. 'Imagine', he said, 'a theatre. You know the play, can recite many of its lines from memory, but you are attending a new production, and suddenly you are assaulted by sensations you had not anticipated.'

Señor Aguilar's metaphor perfectly mirrored what he talked about: the choice of his figure was not original, as he himself knew, though he made no apology for resorting to the familiar image; indeed, the glimmer in his eyes indicated that he was aware of enjoying the position of a critic who knew he himself was the ultimate, and finally the only, object of his own theory, but that was only his way of accommodating his listener: which is to say he made me feel quite at ease for there seemed to be no threat of originality in his speech. Once he had thus drawn me into his confidence, however, he astonished me with a twist in the conversation for which I had been unprepared – in the process perhaps giving me a clue (which I apprehended only in retrospect) that the regular tricks of my storyteller's trade were child's play to him. I had only remarked at the curious phenomenon of the weather; he, seeming to expatiate on that subject, giving me the impression that he was only uttering the usual baroque language which was no more than a civilized complement to the rather pleasant, albeit ordinary, Chilean wine that we drank, subtly transformed the subject and had me – me the novelist and he the critic! – entirely submerged in what he was amused later to hear me refer to as the 'Jamesian great glazed tank of fiction'.

His narrative centred upon the life of an American named Tony Quaglino who had gone to Otavalo in 1969 as an emissary of one of those altruistic bodies, like the Peace Corps, seeking to escape the sense of desolation that tormented his generation, leaving the sooty air of urban New Jersey for what he resignedly expected would be a wilderness but what turned out to be a charming ancient civilization peopled by ruddy-complexioned Indians who grew corn and slaughtered pigs. Señor Aguilar paused after his introductory description of Quaglino – twenty-two years old, dark Italian type, guilty at his good fortune in not being drafted – and leaning forward to place my glass on the table, I recounted briefly the conjectures that had come to my mind with its habit of inventing stories with only the slightest suggestion from life to prompt it. It was to be a story of a discovery of origins. Or about the disenchantment of naïve presumptions concerning a society in its innocence. Or perhaps about spiritual growth? 'Ah, my friend,' Señor Aguilar said, 'you know too much about life which serves you admirably with its terrible dramas for your stories, but what do you know of the soul's residence in darkness?'

I thought the last a rather extravagant phrase in the mouth of a critic famous in South America for his iconoclasm. 'Not at all,' he countered, remaining grim although my expression had been jocular, 'and please let us not concern ourselves with a public mask.' Surely, as my translator, he must understand that I knew nothing about life except for the annual list of precautions my doctor obliged me to take? But Señor Aguilar was no longer in a mood to share a joke and proposed we retire to the living room for it was beginning to be chilly on the terrace. Rising, I observed that the horizon had gone entirely a dark grey. 'Quaglino's story will amaze you,' he said, leading me into the house.

It took us a few minutes to settle ourselves in comfortable leather chairs with a small mahogany table between us. There was first the solemn business of obtaining ice from the kitchen and pouring out tall glasses of Scotch and soda and, of course, it would have been impolite of me had I not, while my host silently prepared the drinks, expressed my admiration for the large Botero painting that hung on the wall, congratulating him from across the room for possessing so fine a picture. It occurred to me that something of Botero's humour was perceptible in the person of Señor Aguilar who, like the artist's figures, was a globular creature. When I had first met him a few years earlier, he had suddenly said, after the small talk between author and translator had been exhausted, 'Ironies attend our birth.' He had proceeded to give an autobiographical example. 'My humble parents, who could not write the language they spoke, named me Próspero, no doubt hoping that I would have better luck in the game of life, little knowing that I was destined to study the language of Shakespeare. But observe this further irony: given an exceptional talent with words, I was not given the magic wand of creation, only a ballpoint pen with which to make marks in the margins of others or to substitute their words with Spanish ones.' He was the translator of my novel, that I had had the temerity, or the foolishness, to entitle *Verónica and the Góngora Passion*, and written in a language that had deliberate affinities with the style of G. K. Chesterton, with a pinch of suspense from Robert Louis Stevenson – a vain attempt to avoid the vulgarity of being considered *modern*, vain because British and American reviewers had ignored the book as one more experimental novel with inflated avant-garde pretensions. My poor Verónica died before she could be born. Señor Aguilar had said excitedly, 'Ah, my ballpoint will yet be a wand!' and made the preposterous proposal that his translation be presented to the Spanish-speaking world as the original, allowing paperback houses in London and New York to bring out their editions as a translation. The critic, I observed to him, was ever an opportunist wanting to usurp the writer's eminence. 'What do you want,' he asked pointedly, 'fame in this life and wealth for your heirs?' I did not understand his question, and he took my puzzled silence to indicate acquiescence in his fatal scheme – in due course, the English-language paperback edition was attacked for the translator's wooden, old-fashioned prose style, and my poor Verónica languishes as an old maid in one culture and drives men crazy with her gaudy whorishness in the other. I walked away from the Botero seeing that my host had placed the two glasses on the small mahogany table and had himself taken a seat next to it, and waited to resume his story.

Of course, Quaglino's earlier experiences in the Ecuadorian interior were merely the predictable impressions of a young American whose only idea of a foreign world was a ten-day tour of Britain during his senior year in high school when without his conscious reflection the idea had been lodged in his mind that landscapes – moist, overcast, misty, the great elm trees a liquid shimmering in the middle distance – were most deeply coloured when they were blurred, the general grey throbbing with an intense vivacity, all blue and green and yellow, but who had flown back to New York and blindly crossed the city and returned home without having the feeling that he had recently left it; so that his arrival in the Andes at first evoked the usual expressions of how charming this new world was, how terribly sharp its edges, how different was its pace – all the trite observations of a young man who was arrogantly convinced that he was experienced in life: had he not witnessed the maturing of his nation, beginning to doubt its role in the world, himself a spokesman for anguish, for repentance in a country where everyone had begun to talk feverishly, passionately; and had he not undergone personal initiations in the underworld of violent sex and drugs when only thirteen and fourteen, and been in the streets when the blacks rioted, smashing the plate-glass security of the fancy stores, setting fires in the nation's blood? His closest friend Jimmy had been drafted and in that tormented time that debauched the young, Jimmy, on the last night before he wore the uniform, rolled his father's blue Mustang from a cliff and sent it smashing among the rocks, and two months later, though it seemed he had only gone the weekend, taken the return flight home, Jimmy was delivered back to his country in a plastic bag. And the young women of his group, hysterical with losing their men to the whore ideology, among them Betsy whom he believed he loved, threw away the old Doris Day Susan Hayward expectations of their mothers' generation, and in the confusion of voices in the militant time, slogans everywhere, revisions of customs, everywhere the shrieking questions and accusations, demanded the male despise himself, and Betsy who, like a pagan bowing before the lingam, had been thrillingly idolatrous in their carnal exchanges, announced to him, standing erect in her black turtleneck and blue jeans, that she would never love a man again.

And, of course, Quaglino's first few months in the new world had been lost in the foreigner's eager exhibitions to be like the natives, strumming a guitar among peasants in a bar, and in expressions of an inflated approval of the indigenous culture. But then Fourth of July nostalgia took him to Quito and the embassy's barbecue and the consular section's amateur country-and-western whining, mildly nourishing at first with flavours of home, triggered the mechanism of diabolical memory, of the stress of being, the brightness of the Andean sky inexplicably befogged in his vision, and he walked without thinking, but driven only to keep moving, gulping the thin air like one trying to allay an attack of nausea, until he arrived in the old city. All churches and preserved houses with geraniums in the window boxes. Iglesia de San Francisco, Iglesia de Santo Domingo, Capilla de las madres de San Diego. He opened the heavy wooden doors into the baroque interiors, columns and altars of gold, of gold the sacred heart on paintings. And there was that picture, the Virgin of the Flowers, the baby in the crook of her right arm, in the gilt frame with the painted frame of flowers around the oval window that revealed the dark interior where she sat, a flower in her left hand, and the child's hand at her breast about to reach for the flower, and Quaglino could not tell why the picture should draw all the air out of his lungs and fill them with black, boiling tar. It was dark in the church. A little murky light from the high begrimed windows seemed more like floating mist than a diffusion of the sun's rays and only served to make the shadows more intense. But the uncanny perception of the soul needs no external illumination and Quaglino, who had seen a blurred greyish landscape become a vivid assault on his vision without remarking upon the curious phenomenon and perhaps had been in the grip of progressive disturbances that, confounding the visible ordinary reality, had been dismissed as aberrations, now felt a severe choking in his throat and at the same time a descent into darkness as if the mind had finally been able to release the spring that unlocked the door to ecstasy but, entering, found itself only in a void.

Quaglino never knew what happened, how he recovered his breath and walked away from the Virgin of the Flowers, from her oppressive innocence, from the fearful beauty of the child, how he left the city and found himself after a time, a moment, a year, that he had no way of measuring, beside a narrow river in a jungle. Who can believe the chronicler of illusions and who, suddenly plunged into fissures that open in the human mind, can doubt the inventor of dreams fabricating the swirling misty forms that are the paradigms of a terrible reality? To remain conscious before a progression of mundane events is a sad burden that we must somehow not buckle under, but from nowhere, or from deep within the soul, comes the unexpected attack and this life is replaced by a memory, the blood that had coursed silently bursts into a million efflorescences, each one a life making a singular claim to the body from which it has been shed. It is a form of a profound distraction of the self, this casual glance that has you staring at the infinite.

A group of girls, six or seven, among them Tamarinha, all recent celebrants of a puberty rite, come to the river to wash off the ceremonious streaks of red urucu paint from their small conical breasts and slender thighs, found him where he lay in a swoon on the bank, smothering the little magenta flowers growing there in a wild profusion. Quaglino felt a shiver in his body hearing the ringing voices of the girls engaged in a boisterous splashing of one another and stood up with a start; in the same moment, the girls noticed him and went dead still, knee-deep in the water, confused and shocked as if there were another aspect of the rite, hitherto kept secret from them, that had still to be performed. But the tallest girl, Tamarinha, spoke, a long flow of guttural speech. Quaglino heard the sound of her voice come rippling in the air, wondered what meaning there must be in her words, but the hissing, squawking phrases flew past him without his being able to catch the significance of a single one. Encouraged by

Tamarinha's boldness, and seeing that the man made no dangerous advance, the other girls began to hoot in a communal derision of the absurdity of his being, and in a moment had leaped out of the river and started to tear off his clothes. It was only when they saw the pale white skin of the naked man that bewilderment came over them, and they looked at one another with unspoken questions and suddenly ran off. Quaglino heard their shrieks as they fled into the darkness of the forest, and he went after them, abandoning his shredded clothes scattered among the trampled flowers. He stopped after a while, panting, noticing that the shrieking had ceased. The jungle was thick around him, long loops of creepers hung from the high trees. There was no path in the undergrowth of ferns where he stood. Not a bird broke the silence for some minutes. Then the twittering began, the voices of the girls warbling in little bursts, making cooing sounds, cackling sounds, now seemingly just behind the tree nearest him and now farther away. Blindly, he pursued the sounds. The voices broke more loudly as he came to the darkest part of the forest. This way, they seemed to cry in a raucous bursting of sound, come, follow quickly! Warm now, the voices of the girls, reaching him in waves of harmony, sibilants stroking his body, and then screechy or riotous or playful, pulling him this way and that, as if they held him with a long cord tied to his waist.

When he found himself come at last to a clearing, he felt a sense of disappointment that it was only a small village with a cluster of a dozen huts that he had arrived at. A group of men and women, dispersing at the conclusion of some ceremony, noticed his appearance with mild curiosity and hardly any astonishment. Beads and macaw feathers adorned their bodies, the men smeared with ashes, the women covered from forehead to feet with geometrical red lines that created optical dislocations in their flesh. Gathered in a group like a receiving party, they stood looking at him as at a long expected dignitary. Quaglino regarded the assembly with composure, experiencing no trepidation to find himself among savages. Indeed, he felt quite relaxed. Pools of light from the high sun breaking through the tall trees fell on the village. The huts were laid out in a circle with one larger edifice at the centre. The fringe of the jungle that could be seen in between the huts was comprised of flowering bushes that, catching the scattered light in the general darkness, emitted an unnaturally bright vividness. A moaning kind of a sound, the undertone of the tribe's speech, rose among the men and the women, turned to a rapid chattering and stopped. Suddenly, the men gave a jubilant cry and rushed toward him. The women, remaining where they were, began to chant. He was taken away to the men's hut, the building at the centre, where he got the impression that he was being treated with a jolly camaraderie, the men slapping his back and speaking to one another in a jovial manner while gesturing toward him with their eyes. A liquor was served and drunk with a great deal of laughter. The thick, creamy liquid seemed odourless and not too potent. The taste was not repulsive, as he had anticipated. Food was sent in. Fish and some root ground and boiled into a mush. Not unpleasant; but as with the drink, he had tasted nothing. More liquor was passed around. The men began to sing, a nasal chanting.

Quaglino felt no apprehension at his situation, and nor any curiosity as to what was about to transpire. To himself, he had become bodiless, a spirit only, his one possession the faculty of perception, which witnessed the shell of his life with the memory echoing in it of another life from which, too, the flesh had fallen: he was in a trance of being, a state not hallucinatory and not the infliction of a devilish curse, but that crossing of light forces in the mind, a projection of beams from several sources, creating where they overlap an unimagined illumination. The self, the soul then resides in darkness, paradoxically as if in the centre of the sun.

He was kept in the men's hut for several weeks. The primitive world was remarkably familiar and without surprises. The men talked to him in their language which he did not understand. He saw them go away fishing or hunting and heard the yells of the children when they returned with a catch. The women sat pounding roots outside their huts, or weaving baskets and hammocks. He was not even surprised by the extraordinary amount of ennui that the tribe had to bear, days of listlessness and unexpressed dolour.

When some prescribed duration of time had passed, when the shaman had counted so many swellings of the moon, so many afternoons when the clouds took on the shapes of beasts of prey and devoured the sky, a procession playing on home-made percussion instruments led Quaglino from the men's hut some distance to a wide pond full of water-lilies and yellow hyacinths. There he was bathed, and emerging with refreshened eyes, with cooler breath, he saw beyond the chanting crowd of men the bushes and trees covered with flowers, trumpeting red blossoms and little purses of purple petals, and behind a group of yellow acacias a field of magenta flowers. Returning to the village, he was given a hut of his own where the women daily hung garlands of flowers across its open front to form a curtain. He smelled nothing, however, and tasted nothing, though food and drink were brought to him and the flowers were sprinkled at noon with water from the pond.

When another prescribed duration of time had passed, when the black clouds that brought torrential rains came no more and steam rose from the land under the noonday sun, the village commenced a celebration, eating the abundant fish from the swollen rivers, that ended on the fifth day with a procession that brought Tamarinha to his hut, her body painted with urucu, red triangles and circles all over her skin. He understood that he was being married to her, that she was his bride in the dark world, his virgin under the canopy of the jungle, that his coming to the tribe had been a portent, making him the messenger of potency, the agent of rebirth: in this bodiless life, in this casual sojourn within memory, he was the creator, his non-being the vessel from which must pour a vital reincarnation.

The son was born. In that unreal existence, as if the tribe around him was made up of figures in an anthropological study, his brain preoccupied itself with memories of another life – the rust spots on the door of the Mustang that he noticed just when Jimmy was letting the car roll to the edge of the cliff, the festive decorations in the store windows on Fifth Avenue each December when his parents took him to New York to see the bright lights, the Saturday nights smoking pot among compacted cars in a junk yard in Newark near a foul-smelling canal that carried industrial effluence to the river. A million details evoked again the reality and the fiction of a time now dead. Betsy had said, cruelly he then thought, 'I have better things to do with my life than become a breeder.' He had innocently asked, 'Such as?' She had looked scornfully at him and answered in a harsh voice, 'The planet's fucked, don't you realize that?' And pausing, staring at him with increasing scorn, she had added, 'By *man*!' He was stunned that the vengeance taught her by her lately espoused rhetoric should unaccountably make him a particular victim. And his friend Dennis, who was dead set on enlisting if he did not get drafted, had said on being called up, 'We should bomb them out of sight!' And added in his bellicose enthusiasm, 'Russia and China, too!' Simon who was with them and who had realized that day that his resolution to escape to Canada would have to be carried out, had said weakly, 'Come on, you can't mean that.' Dennis had replied, 'We've got the power, man, we've got the technology.' Simon sighed and looked at Dennis in despair, saying in a soft voice, 'Didn't you read about Lake Eerie? Christ, technology isn't going to save us, *it* is the problem.' Thus the echoes of chaos, of desperate passions, of accumulated guilts; thus the voices addicted to hope, to change; thus the fragmentation of that reality in his mind. But around him, Quaglino heard the alien voices chanting in celebration, saw processions of women at dawn and at dusk, their arms laden with flowers, come and deck the hut in which Tamarinha lay in the hammock with her child, and watched the tribe feast in jubilation. His memories of the other life, rehearsed in his own language, were more vivid than his immediate experience which, as if happening to another, was not burdened by the torment of time and therefore passed without his senses being engaged. He remembered his months with Betsy before she changed her conviction, recalling in detail their love-making, but Tamarinha became a blank as soon as he turned his eyes away from her. The thought again came to him that he was simply not present in his body. And yet the son had been born and the birth the occasion for the tribe's enduring joy.

He was walking back one afternoon from the men's hut where he had been especially feasted and saw from a distance that the garlands of flowers hanging at the front of Tamarinha's hut formed a rectangular frame; going closer, he observed that clusters of smaller flowers on the inner edge of the frame created the effect of an oval window. Inside this window, Tamarinha was to be seen sitting in the hammock, the baby on her right thigh, with her right hand coming round the baby's back to support it, and her head leaning toward the baby's head where it rested against her right shoulder. Her eyes looked down on the flower that she held in her left hand as though she were offering it to the baby whose right hand, resting on her breast, seemed about to move to accept the flower. At Tamarinha's back, the two ends of the hammock described a perfect semi-circle, but the light entering the hut gave the impression of continuing the curving line so that he saw a complete circle, the whole a diffused disc behind the mother and the child. A shudder ran through Quaglino's body that was a throbbing of a re-awakening consciousness, and a blackness stormed into his brain as if his lungs had collapsed.

Señor Aguilar remained silent for several minutes. Then he shook his head and said, 'The horror of such a life! The thought that had come to Quaglino's mind just before the blackness overwhelmed him was a shocking one, too abominable to utter. God forgive me if I must utter it, for without it Quaglino's story has no meaning. I derive some comfort from the fact that the vile, profane words are Quaglino's and not mine and it is with loathing, with terror, that I speak them: *Evil began with God*.'

I did not break the silence that again filled the room. On the wall, Botero's rotund figures smiled placidly in their ballooned world while my globular companion sat in a state of spiritual dejection brought on by the appalling narrative. Outside, it was completely dark. The fog was undoubtedly thick. But I remained silent not because I had been shocked by the ending of the story. Señor Aguilar had said I would be amazed by it, but he could not have suspected in what manner. The contract with the Buenos Aires publisher was still being negotiated; I had only the previous day, on my arrival, presented Señor Aguilar with a copy of the novella that, with my usual recklessness with titles, was called *The American and the Virgin*; and so far, Señor Aguilar, preoccupied with entertaining me, had not had the opportunity to go beyond touching the pages and performing the gracious gesture of gently removing the dust-cover with its lurid illustration and passing his fingertips over the black cloth in which the slight volume was bound in order to express his delight in American book-binding: in brief, he did not know the contents of the book, and yet he seemed already to know my story by heart.

THE CHILD AND THE POET

Rachel Gould

'Growing up', said the teacher, 'is an imaginary process.' She paused to give someone time to ask, 'Do you mean a process of the imagination, or a process that doesn't really exist?'

Unfortunately the question was only in her own mind – no one actually asked it, as she was teaching a class of eleven-year-olds, and no one could really expect – though she did – eleven-year-olds to ask questions of such sophistication. She stared for a moment with a feeling of indignation at the twenty-two faces staring at her, not one of whose mouths was even on the point of opening to ask any question at all. It was likely that they hadn't understood her sentence, let alone appreciated its ambiguity.

'An imaginary process,' she repeated. This was her first job since leaving training college, and she was still firmly of the opinion that children must not be treated as ignorant inexperienced beings, but as minds that will fill to expand all the space that you allow them. She gave them enormous space: the space of her own experience, her own passionate feelings, all her very wide reading and the even wider sweep of ideas that that reading provoked in her, but the main result seemed to be – after a half term of teaching – that the class considered her mad. Occasionally she felt ready to admit defeat – giving the benefit of the doubt was all very well, but she did not want to be a fool – but whenever she saw a silly sentimental woman leaning over a pram dribbling baby language into it (which is a common sight everywhere) she felt the same revulsion she had always felt, and determined to give the benefit of the doubt until the absolutely most bitter end if need be. What the absolutely most bitter end might be she was not sure, but she supposed it would be the moment when the children became so convinced of her madness that they complained to their parents or to the headmaster, and she lost her job.

'And that is *why*', she said, in tones of triumph which she was far from feeling, 'literature is so important. I won't for the moment go into the question of what constitutes literature, as that is a matter of some debate in academic circles: let us suppose that literature means simply books, although in fact it is only some books, and also I suppose includes some things which you could hardly call books, as they are simply manuscripts on vellum, unbound, and not what we nowadays consider to be a book. But, anyway, since Caxton established the first printing press in this country – have you done that yet in history? – which he did in the sixteenth century, as I remember, literature has mostly been in books. Does anyone know what was the first book ever to be published in England?'

Silence.

'Well, to the best of my remembrance – which is not utterly reliable, but I think this is right: ask your parents when you get home – it was Sir Thomas Malory's Morte d'Arthur, which is French, and means, the death of Arthur. Arthur was a king of Britain – a mythical king of Britain, though perhaps based on some small historical counterpart – who is supposed to be lying now in a Welsh cave with all his knights, sleeping, waiting for the moment to come and save Britain – which, God knows, we need. But I can't tell you his story now. If you're interested, remind me later in the term when we have nothing in particular to do, and I will tell you.'

A boy at the back of the class put up his hand.

'Yes, Calvin?'

'Miss,' he said, 'I thought you were going to tell us why literature is so important.'

'I'm glad you asked me that, Calvin. I was going to tell you, and it shows that you were following the train of my thought very closely, and have noticed that we had got a little side-tracked. Not that side-tracking is a bad thing, in my opinion, as one often discovers things on a side-track that one had no idea were there. However, yes. Literature is terribly important because of what I said at the beginning of the lesson – that growing up is an imaginary process. You are all growing up, and even I, though to you I must seem already grown-up, am still growing up. Even very old people, or at least, the best of them, are still growing up.'

'Miss,' said a girl in the second row. 'Is Mr Claxson still growing up?'

Mr Claxson was the headmaster, who was coming up to retirement.

'Well, to be quite frank with you – but this is something you shouldn't repeat – I'm fairly certain that he hardly grew up at all. He probably stopped before he was as old as you are. I mean, he went on growing physically, obviously, but as for his mind, I think that stopped growing at a very early stage: shall we say, a premature stage.'

'Is that why he's always so boring in prayers?'

'Yes, exactly. And also, to be fair to him, because a headmaster's job is a very boring one – it is so bound up with administration, with organising things, I mean, and he doesn't have the benefit of teaching you, whose fresh minds might make him a little un-boring again.'

The children looked at each other and smiled with satisfaction at the idea of their fresh minds.

'But the main reason is probably – to get back to Calvin's prompt, as he's looking as though he suspects me of side-tracking again – that he never understood the connection between growing up and literature. The connection is, that growing up is to do with what one learns from one's experience . . . You all know what experience is, do you?'

'What happens to you?'

'What happens to you, exactly. That is a very good definition. Well, the point is that by reading books, you can gain vicariously – which means sort of in a sideways way, by substitution, as though you were the person in the book – the experiences of all the people you read about, and that means that you can grow up much quicker than you would if you had to wait for all those things actually to happen to you, so that you could learn from them, and also much wider than you might otherwise do – because there might be things you'd read about which never would happen to you, even if you waited your whole lives. For example, however long you waited, you probably wouldn't sail on a huge sailing ship, because they don't exist much nowadays, but by reading – Robinson Crusoe, which you all must know about, or Moby Dick, which is about a whaling ship – you can find out. So literature makes you use your imagination – I mean, it makes you think about things that don't actually exist here and now – and so you enter into someone else's thoughts and feelings, and you grow to understand them better; you grow up. As a child, there are many things that are difficult to understand, but even for adults, even though in general they're more grown-up and understand more things, there still are things which are difficult to understand clearly.'

'What sort of things, Miss?'

She felt that the benefit of the doubt was beginning to pay off in this lesson, for any child who could ask that question could not be stupid. Although perhaps, just conceivably, he was what the children called a 'stirrer' – someone who says things to provoke. She was not at all provoked, however.

'Well, things like ... the existence or otherwise of God, and morals – which is the whole question of what things are right and what things are wrong, and even, whether there is such a thing as right and wrong – although that is more a question for moral philosophy. I don't expect that you've thought much yet about whether God exists ...' There was a general shaking of heads. '... but you must already have noticed that it's difficult to distinguish always between right and wrong.'

There were looks of perplexity on some faces.

'Well, I'll give you an example then. Your mother comes into your bedroom just before she's going out with your father, and she asks you if you like her dress. Well, you happen to think that her dress is absolutely disgusting, but you know it's supposed to be a 'best' dress, and that she will be very hurt if you tell her that you don't like it. Do you see what I mean? Should you tell a lie? Or should you tell the truth and hurt your mother, who wants to feel that she looks as pretty as she can look? That, of course, is a fairly minor example, but when one grows up there are some quite important problems of that sort of difficulty.'

She might now have been a little provoked if any child had asked her for a specific example of this sort of quite important difficult problem, but luckily their curiosity about specifics seemed to have been satisfied for the moment.

'Anyway, we must get back to literature and growing up. It is because I think this about literature and growing up that I chose to teach English, and to teach children of your age. Of course, I could have taught French or German or even Swahili, but then I would probably have had to teach children older than you.'

'And why didn't you want to, Miss?'

'Well, because children of your age are more influenceable. Someone said – I can't remember off-hand who – 'Give me a child at a tender age, and he is mine for life.' (Or she, of course.)'

'What did they mean by tender?'

'They meant young, like young shoots of plants, which are very tender. And the point is that because you are as young as you are, your minds are soft and malleable – which means I can shape them how I like, like plasticine – but on the other hand, because you are eleven, you're just about old enough to understand books which aren't really children's books – like Alice in Wonderland, or Treasure Island, or The Would-be-goods, who are Victorian children who are somehow always getting into scrapes. Perhaps during the course of the year we will read some of them, too . . . although the year is beginning to look a little small for all the things I want to do.'

'However, all this has just been a little preamble to the main point of the lesson, which is the poem we're going to look at. Do any of you read poems at all, or have them read to you by your parents?'

One or two children nodded.

'That's good. I suppose anyway most of you know nursery rhymes, which are a sort of poem – but most of those weren't written by anyone in particular. They're what's called 'traditional', which means they sort of grew up, vaguely, and were passed on by word of mouth. But the poem we're going to look at was written by someone in particular. The problem about poetry is that children get the idea it is something you only read in school, but I want you to imagine that the person who wrote this wasn't writing it in a dry way, to be read without enthusiasm in a school book – he was writing because he had a strong feeling which he wanted to get down on paper and pass on to other people – to his friends, for example, or to his family, and eventually (but only eventually) to people who would read it in a book when it was published. And those people went out and bought the book because they liked to know about other people's strong feelings and opinions – they wanted to know more than they knew already, they wanted to understand other people, they wanted to grow up as much as they possibly could – so that their minds would be like the beanstalk in Jack and the Beanstalk, which grows up and up into the clouds and even higher, into heaven. That's how big the imagination can be, you see, if you feed it properly, like feeding a beanstalk with manure and compost, with the things that imagination grows from.'

Some of the children were staring up right through the ceiling, not from boredom – far from it – but as though seeing the beanstalk with all its tendrils and clusters of red flowers, growing up and up. Calvin, in particular, had an odd smile on his face, one which gave his teacher a great deal of satisfaction, and seemed lost in contemplation of the wonderful plant. The teacher smiled silently as she turned to the blackboard and picked up a long piece of chalk. She was more disposed to give the benefit of the doubt to Calvin Smith than to any other child in her class, and on this point was in complete disagreement with all the other teachers in the school, except for the art master. In the opinion of the others, he was at best a dreamer, at worst lazy and lacking in application.

'Now,' she said, 'I'm going to write the poem out on the board, and I'd like you to copy it out in your books. This may seem boring to you, but I'd like you to imagine that you are *writing* the poem – for the first time. It's you who are thinking of the words to put down: you're choosing each one, specially, instead of another, because it's the one that seems to fit best. Then I think you'll understand a bit what it's like to write a poem. So I don't want you to rush at it – take your time and think hard about each word. Imagine they're sweets, suck them very slowly and let the taste trickle down your throats.'

There was silence for a time, except for occasional squeakings of chalk as the teacher wrote the poem on the board in an italic hand so clear and regular that it seemed to belie the wilder flights of her fancy, the beanstalk, King Arthur and the rest. The children bent over their exercise books, lifting and lowering their heads in an unco-ordinated rhythm which reminded the teacher, as she glanced at them briefly to check that they were concentrating as they should, of some wooden chickens she had had as a child, which bent over to peck corn at the pull of a handle. When she had finished, she sat down and began marking some exercise books.

A girl came up to her desk to sharpen a pencil in the old-fashioned sharpener screwed like a meat-mincing machine to the teacher's desk-edge; she smiled at the girl, whose writing was bad and who needed encouragement. Then behind the girl she noticed Calvin with a look of fading patience on his face, one arm in the air held there by the other at the elbow – a position the children adopted when they felt they were in for a long wait.

'Yes, Calvin?'

'Miss,' he said, 'I think it's a bit wrong.'

'What is?'

'The poem.'

'You mean, I've made a mistake copying it onto the board?'

'Yes, Miss.'

'Do you know the poem then, Calvin?'

Calvin looked puzzled. He screwed his eyes up and glanced down at his exercise book where his poem stopped in mid-line at the word 'Yet'.

'No, I don't think so, no. I've just got a feeling . . .' He stopped, and looked at the teacher questioningly.

'A feeling about what? Don't be shy – I often have feelings like that about things. Perhaps someone read it to you once when you were smaller, and you've remembered deep down; it's quite a famous poem as poems go. And it's quite likely I've made a mistake in the copying – people often did, when they had to copy everything by hand, before printing. Lucky for the academics, who can discuss interminably which word is most likely to be right.'

'But it isn't just one word – it's a whole line.'

'Oh.' She turned and looked at the poem she had written on the board. 'Well, I don't think I can have got a whole line wrong in such a small poem. Which line, Calvin?'

'The one about in the middle, that begins with 'Yet'.'

'And what did you think it should be?'

'Well, I thought it should be . . .' Here he paused for several seconds, so that the teacher assumed that what would follow would be a few halting words, a misremembered jumble.

'I thought it was, 'Yet could I never judge what men could mean', and then, 'Till I heard . . .' like you've got.'

The teacher looked at Calvin with thinly-disguised admiration; then, recovering herself, she said, 'That does fit the metre. I mean, it has the right number of syllables, the right pattern – pom, pom, pom . . .' She found it difficult to explain grammar and prosody to children who had no formal training in either. 'But that's not what I've got in my book. I'll look this evening when I get home – this edition doesn't have any notes.

'Have the rest of you finished copying it down?'

'Not *yet*, Miss,' said the girl who had come up to sharpen her pencil.

'Well, go on, then. And try and think, really *think*, what it's like to write each word – whether the words are strange, or simple, or poetic . . . Then we'll talk about that in a minute.'

Calvin chewed the top of his pencil a little before bending his head with the others' and continuing his poem. The teacher, who went back to her marking, did not notice that the smile which had hovered over his face as he took in the height and twisting tendrils of the beanstalk had now completely disappeared. He made no further contribution to the lesson, and his expression was the mask of weary boredom that the other teachers in the school knew so well.

'Now, can anyone tell me what the poem is about?'

There was a new silence. Calvin could probably have said, but wouldn't.

'Does anyone know who Homer is?'

The silence lengthened, and in it came the sound of heavy masculine footsteps along the corridor outside the classroom. Mr Claxson appeared at the door, where he was scrutinised by the children with an interest he did not normally command: they were looking for signs of his stunted growth. The teacher smiled conspiratorially and put her finger to her lips, and the children – as though this were a pre-arranged signal – got up and chorused, 'Good afternoon, Mr Claxson.' The headmaster waved them jovially back into their seats. 'Good afternoon, children; good afternoon, Miss Tustian. Just thought I'd drop in and see how your class was going, Miss Tustian. Do so enjoy seeing what newfangled devices have been invented for the inculcation of information into young brains. Fascinating, fascinating. Always enjoyed English very much – never understood why I chose to teach mathematics. Dreary subject, some say. Quite so, quite . . . but I digress. Please, do go on. I'll sit down here.'

'I was just asking the class if they knew who Homer was,' said Miss Tustian.

'And do they?' asked the headmaster, tactlessly, pulling his trouser-legs carefully up to mid-calf so that they would not bag at the knees.

A 'no' hovered on the teacher's lips for a long precarious moment, and then a girl's voice said nervously, 'Miss, is he a book?'

'Not exactly a book, Em, but a person who wrote a book, or rather, two: The Iliad and The Odyssey. But we do say 'Homer' as though he were a book, as we say 'Shakespear' meaning all his plays – as though the person and the things he wrote were the same. Homer was a Greek, who wrote hundreds of years before Jesus was born. His poems were traditional too, like the nursery rhymes I was talking about earlier, but he was the first person to write them down. At least, that's what people think . . .' She would have liked to explain about oral poetry and how Homer might not be one person but several, but there were only ten minutes to go before the end of the class, there was no time – she had yet to get on to the poem proper.

'Anyway,' she drew a long breath, 'The Iliad and The Odyssey are the earliest works in Greek literature – the earliest we know of, at any rate – and they are what this poem is about. Now you know that, can you tell me what the poem is saying about Homer?'

'Miss, who is Chapman then?'

'My mother was called Chapman before she got married,' a boy offered from the back of the room. Miss Tustian remained unflustered.

'Yes, it's a very English name – and very old too, obviously. Chapman is the name of the man who first translated Homer into English, because of course Homer wrote in Greek. So what does the poet mean in the title when he says 'on first looking into'?'

'Has he been reading it, Miss?'

'Yes, he has. And how many times has he read Homer before?'

'Never.'

'Never. Exactly. You see, these are some of the most famous poems in the world, and he says that he's often been told about them, but he's never read them before. And now he's just read part for the very first time, and he thinks it's so tremendous that he's sat down and written a poem about it. What happened was that he went round to a friend's house one evening, and read Chapman's Homer there, and then he walked back very late at night from the City across the river to where he lived, near London Bridge Station (except that the station wasn't there then) – he was thinking and thinking about Homer, and when he got back he'd formed a poem in his head, and he sat down and wrote the poem straight off. *This* poem.'

The children looked harder at the poem on the board.

'You mean, he lived in London, Miss?'

'Yes.'

'Very near here,' muttered Calvin under his breath, but no one heard him.

The children were watching a young man striding across a bridge in their London, in the dark, very fast – he was in a hurry. Under him the river glittered occasionally, catching the flare of the gas-lamps, and his head was full of Homer and his own poem coming to life slowly winding round Homer like honeysuckle.

'You see how excited he is?' their teacher asked. 'And he wants you to know, to feel what it's like to discover a new place – he talks about books as though they were places, and each new place has a different landscape: different hills, different skies, different plants, a different light. And what does he say at the end about how he feels, discovering this new country?'

'Like an astronomer.'

'Yes. And like Cortez, who was one of the Spaniards who came to the Americas after they'd been discovered by Christopher Columbus – who was the first man from our part of the world to cross to the other side and see the Pacific: a whole huge ocean that they didn't know was there. You see what effect it has on them? They've been trecking across country for days on foot – or perhaps Cortez had a horse, as he was commander – through thick green wild forests, with monkeys chattering and weird-coloured birds screeching in the trees – parrots perhaps . . . would there have been parrots, Mr Claxson?'

'I'm afraid I really don't know, my dear Miss Tustian. But parrots sound very apposite, very apposite indeed . . .'

'And then the trees begin to thin out, they climb a hill, or a mountain – that's the peak in Darien – and as they reach the skyline, there, suddenly, is a huge sea, with breakers rolling in on white beaches, and spreading out and out further than their eyes can see, into a blue haze in the distance. And they turn and stare at each other with their mouths open, astonished.' She laughed. 'Just as you're all doing now.' The children laughed too at the expressions on each other's faces. Parrots, whether apposite or not, would always be caged for them in that poem now, flitting in gorgeous streaks of pink and scarlet and citrus-yellow behind Homer and Chapman and stout Cortez.

'And do you see how this poem connects with what I was saying at thc beginning of the lesson? About literature and growing up? He's elated, he's drunk almost, but instead of with drink – which makes you feel sleepy, befuddled – with words; he feels that he's grown – he's the discoverer of a new planet, and a conquistador, a conqueror of new lands. But also he feels dwarfed by the immensity of what he's discovered – it gives him a sense of his relative size, like the men with Cortez who are struck dumb by the hugeness of the Pacific. That's what you can learn from . . .'

Here the teacher's words, which had been pouring out with ever-increasing speed and enthusiasm in the race against time – always lost – were stridently cut off by the school bell marking the end of the day's lessons.

'Oh,' said Miss Tustian with quiet disappointment. 'Well, we'll go back to it tomorrow.'

'Miss, we don't *have* English tomorrow. We have double maths and *games* tomorrow.'

'So you do. On Thursday, then. And try not to be late for registration tomorrow, any of you.'

She doubted whether they heard this last admonition as they stuffed exercise and text books into their satchels, glancing at the clock and estimating how fast they would have to run to catch the first of the two school buses.

The headmaster came up to the teacher's desk. 'May I help you carry those books to the staff room, Miss Tustian?' he asked. 'That's very kind of you, Mr Claxson,' she said, with self-conscious formality. 'Thank you.'

Mr Claxson held the door open for the most recently-appointed and youngest teacher in his school, and as they disappeared down the corridor in the direction of the staff room his voice could be heard saying, 'You have a very ambitious approach to your class, Miss Tustian – you pitch the level very high. Fascinating, most enjoyable. But do you feel they are ready for the classics?'

As Miss Tustian passed through the school gates on her way home – she did not yet have a car, though she hoped to, soon – she overheard, 'And did you have a good day at school, dear?' The mother of one of her pupils was standing over him, straightening his tie and patting down his hair in an attempt to make him look respectable for the voyage home. The boy's eyes were fixed on the pavement during this ignominy, which was a daily event. 'And what did you learn about?'

'About parrots,' said the boy, with a flash of rebelliousness.

'Was that biology? We only ever did slow worms. Aren't you lucky these days. Parrots! We didn't see a banana, or even an orange, till after the war was over.'

The teacher smiled to herself at this non-sequitur, whose logic she perfectly understood.

At the next corner she caught sight of a small figure standing on tip-toe peering over the wall through the wire netting of the netball court where some of the older girls were playing a practice match. Calvin was one of the shortest boys in her class and – as her class were among the youngest – in the whole school, a fact of which he was aggressively aware.

He half-turned his head towards her as she approached and then turned back to watch the game.

'Hello, Calvin,' she said.

'Hello.'

She had noticed before that outside school hours he never called her Miss; she wondered if she could ask him to call her by her Christian name, but thought he might be embarrassed. He was easily embarrassed.

'Are you going home my way?' she asked. They had walked part of the way home together once or twice before; he seemed to enjoy talking, and unlike the rest of her class – who tended to ignore her if they met her outside school – he didn't feel constrained because she was his teacher.

'Not today,' he said, adding, 'I . . . I'm waiting for someone,' by way of explanation.

'Ah. Well, I'll see you tomorrow then.'

'Yes,' said Calvin.

She felt a little disappointed, and then, as she transferred her brief-case from one hand to the other, somewhat absurd that she should be disappointed by the temporary withdrawal of friendship of an eleven-year-old boy. And then she began to watch what was going on around her: the women out with wicker baskets on wheels for a last few things before the shops shut, the pyramids of fruit glowing from the long heat of the day, the fitting of a new green-and-white striped sun awning – exactly like the old one, but startlingly clean – to the old-fashioned fish shop in the high street, and forgot everything else.

Towards the end of her habitual route home there was a long strip of waste land running beside the river, boarded off from the streets with rusting corrugated iron. Whatever had been demolished there – warehouses, probably – had gone a long time ago, and the patch of land was now an undulating riot of weeds and buddleia. The buddleias had grown wherever their roots could lodge in the powdery foundations: some were tiny bushes, others more than six feet high, and all were in flower with drooping tassels of dark purple. The usual green of the wilderness had been obliterated in the last weeks by the pink rods of rosebay willow herb, all of them bent now in the same direction by a soft but persistent wind. She stopped, as she often did, at one of the places where the metal had been bent back from the wooden stakes that supported it, and looked across the rich blur of pink and purple at the silhouette of Tower Bridge.

From the blur, after a moment, appeared a figure climbing out of one of the hollows, a slight figure – Calvin, she was almost sure. Whoever he had been waiting for had apparently not turned up, for he was alone, and switching at the tallest flowers with a long twig. She watched him for a little, and then felt she was spying on something private, and turned away home.

Calvin was carrying on an animated conversation: 'Did you *like* London then?', emphasising 'like' with a long and carefully-judged swipe, and catching the decapitated flower-head as it fell.

'Sometimes I do, yes. But not this part. This part stinks with candle wax from that shop on St Thomas's Street.'

'I don't know that,' said Calvin. 'Perhaps it's gone. A lot has. But don't you like smells? I do. I like the smell of the river, for example, when the tide goes out and you can see all the mud flats like the sludge at the bottom of a mug of cocoa when it's made properly thick. It still has a smell when the tide's up, too – do you notice that? Very faint. It's best to go down there in the dark, then you smell it most clearly – like a green fog, like cold washing up water. I go fishing down there sometimes. Not with a real rod – I made one out of a good straight stick I found. Never caught anything very much though.' He gave a regretful swipe at another flower. 'Sorry,' he said. 'Almost hit you then!' Feeling that perhaps he had been hogging the conversation, he asked, 'Did you go fishing, ever?'

'I don't often, no. Tom did when he was younger. He'd come back spattered with mud. I take more care over how I look.'

'Hmmm . . . pernickety. That's a good word. Pernickety, aren't you?' He thought that might have been a little rude, and reverted to the river.

'You don't catch much because the river's polluted. There used to be salmon, but not any more. Perhaps there were when you were here. And that's another thing I like – the oil slicks. Well, not slicks – just small patches, really. The colours are wonderful – like pigeons' collars, but more gleamy.'

The conversation faltered; 'gleamy' had been a little extravagant. Calvin made a grimace of concentration, looking for a new topic. Several tall willow herbs, ideal subjects for Calvin's flailing stick, were passed, undestroyed. He had thrown the stick away, and was jumping from tussock to tussock, his satchel bumping against his hip.

'You should go to the sea,' the other said. 'That beats

any river.'

'Yes,' said Calvin, humbly. 'I want to go – I've never been.'

'I've just been, for the first time. It was . . .'

'Ace,' suggested Calvin.

'Ace?'

'Amazing, wonderful, superb.'

'Yes, it was. Cliffs – rocks carved in strange shapes by the waves – the huge sea falling over itself all the time at the edge, and wind, and miles and miles of grass cropped very short by the sheep: springy grass that feels as though it's never been walked on before.'

'Yes,' said Calvin again, looking down at the tussock he was standing on, 'I want to go. Perhaps next summer. Perhaps then I can go.'

'Vincent Pritchet?'

'Yes, Miss.'

'Emma Robertson?'

'Yes, Miss.'

'Terry Smart?'

'Yes, Miss.'

'Calvin Smith?'

Silence.

'Calvin?' The teacher lifted her head from the register. 'Is he late *again*?' She felt particularly annoyed that he should be late this morning, on a day when she wasn't teaching him, and when she had something she wanted to talk to him about. 'Bother,' she said to herself.

'Winston Thomas?'

'Yes, Miss.'

'Winifred . . .'

At this moment Mr Claxson appeared suddenly in the doorway. It was a mark of his agitation that he had forgotten to knock – an unusual breach of his normally perfect manners.

'Miss Tustian, I wonder if you would come outside a moment?'

'Of course.'

She followed the headmaster a little way down the corridor.

'It's Calvin Smith, Miss Tustian. He seems to have been beaten up on the way to school – he won't tell me by whom. He is a *stubborn* boy.' Mr Claxson said this with marked disapproval. 'I've left him sitting in the hall. His nose is bleeding rather badly, and I think perhaps he ought to be taken to hospital to check that it isn't broken. I thought you might go with him now, and I shall wait with your class until their first lesson.'

She found Calvin sitting in the assembly hall, holding a large and rather grubby handkerchief to his nose, which was beginning to swell. One of his knees was skinned and he was bending over picking bits of gravel out of it.

'Hello, Calvin,' she said.

'Hello, Miss.' He looked up; pale, but not as battered as Mr Claxson's agitation had led her to expect.

'Mr Claxson wants me to take you to out-patients to check that your nose isn't broken.'

'Oh, Miss. Do we have to? I don't want any fuss. It'll stop bleeding in a minute.'

'Maybe. But if it's broken it ought to be seen to quickly. You don't want to look like a veteran prize-fighter for the rest of your life, do you?'

'I might,' said Calvin, perversely.

'Well, your parents might not appreciate it in quite the same way.'

'It's *my* nose.'

'What happened, anyway? Did you have a fight?'

Calvin stared at her morosely over his handkerchief. 'Yes, I suppose you could call it that. I didn't start it though.'

'I didn't imagine you had.'

'I was coming through that waste strip, the one down by the river, and they jumped on me.'

'They who? Was it those two from 4c?'

Calvin took his handkerchief away from his nose and looked interestedly at the blood.

'It's not very red, is it?'

'Were you doing anything particularly provocative?'

'They called me short-arse, and a wimp.'

'Ah,' said Miss Tustian. 'What's a wimp?'

'A wimp? It's . . . a wet, a teacher's pet . . . it's a bit difficult to explain.'

'And what were you doing that was wimpish?' she asked.

'I – nothing really. Well, I was talking to myself, like in a play, you know? Sort of acting.'

'Ah,' said the teacher again. 'Well, it's a better excuse for lateness than usual, I suppose. I wanted to ask you about something this morning, you see. You know that line – the one you thought I'd got wrong yesterday. I looked it up last night when I got back, and do you know what it was?'

'No,' said Calvin, examining his bloody handkerchief again.

'The line you said was what he had originally written, and that was how it was first printed. He changed it when the poem was used in a book, later.'

'Ah,' said Calvin.

'Is that all? 'Ah'? How did you know? Your father doesn't collect nineteenth-century magazines, does he?'

'I don't think so. We don't have many books at home. I get them from the library if I need any,' said Calvin.

The teacher looked at him very hard.

'Do you know, Calvin – you're a strange child?'

'No stranger than you are,' said Calvin, quite unabashed.

'No.' She smiled. 'No, probably not.'

DREAMS OF UNFAIR WOMEN

Frank Tuohy

Ted had been silent quite long enough, and so when they stopped at some traffic lights Wanda, who was driving, turned to speak to him.

'What did you think? The meeting, I mean.'

The local branch meeting had taken place in a fine Victorian villa, not far from the sea front. Ted and Wanda were now returning to their rented house, which was on the edge of the town near the university, where he had recently been appointed Lecturer in Social Studies.

'We knew what it was goin' to be like, din't we?'

Wanda had never imitated his attempt at a plebeian accent and, without his Marxist training, always found things less inevitable than he did. 'What way?'

Ted scratched his beard and said: 'They're typical. I min, they sold out, din't they? What else you expect, down here?'

Wanda let in the clutch and drove on, rather fast. Perhaps she had again been too naive and hopeful. She did not want to reject the meeting – or any meeting for that matter – so easily. True, the owner of the house they'd been in had seemed rather pompous. He was Ralph Whittingham, the former Labour MP – 'Call me 'Ralph' with an 'l', please, not 'Rafe'.' However, Wanda had got on well with his wife, an austere woman with her hair in a bun, wearing an ethnic robe of some sort. Mrs Whittingham, it turned out, was a JP, who took a special interest in children 'at risk'. This was one of Wanda's own concerns – though she herself, of course, referred to them as 'kids'.

All the same, Ted was right about one thing: you could not get over the fact that Barmouth was a safe Tory seat and likely to remain one in the future.

'I thought Ron Eastman spoke well,' she said.

Ted snorted. 'He didn't know what he was lettin' himself in for. How many union members can there be down here?'

'Retired ones surely.' Ted snorted again and she went on: 'Probably it's the only chance we'll get of meeting progressive people outside the university.'

Wanda was by nature optimistic, but she had opposed the move to Barmouth in the first place. She had the sort of friends who called it the 'Costa Geriatrica'. Fortunately both their own kids were still at pre-school age. She hoped that in a few years' time Ted would get a better job in London, where Jake and Tamsin would attend a comprehensive with a representative racial mix. Meanwhile, one had to find all the opportunities one could for worthwhile activities. Already in Barmouth she was active in pro-abortion and anti-bomb movements, as well as the problems of pollution, conservation and factory-farming which are always waiting to be taken up.

When Wanda and Ted, two serious-minded children of the middle classes, had first met at the Cambridge University Labour Club, he was looking forward to a career in politics. Somehow his ambition had become less urgent recently. Perhaps he felt isolated without his gang of friends, all of whom still carried around the unsurprising package of attitudes acquired at Cambridge. Unfortunately, Ted didn't get on easily with people who disagreed with him.

But she did not know that Ted had dreams. He had never told her, because he was ashamed of them. Not because his dreams were bad in any conventional sense. While in progress, they were sometimes extremely pleasant. Nor were they really sexual: at least, there was no fantasized betrayal of Wanda, curled beside him in innocent oblivion. Yet after his dreams he woke shuddering with guilt. Being bearded at this stage of his life, he did not have to confront himself in a shaving mirror each morning. Had this been necessary, he didn't think he would have been able to face his own gaze.

Poor Ted, his dreams were of social ambition, naked, horrifying, humbling, grovelling.

That night, after Wanda had made their bedtime cups of tea, sleep shot him back to the Whittingham house in Victorian Barmouth. Unconsciously he had absorbed the upper-middle-class good taste of the surroundings, the Georgian furniture, the varnished paintings that had a valuable air. Against this background there he was, not in his lecturer's garb of jeans and wind-cheater, but pin-striped, drinking tea from porcelain, fervently agreeing with a tidied-up version of Mrs Whittingham that what 'these people' needed was discipline, that social problems were the fault of those that suffered from them. What, we all wondered, had happened to the old values (which meant having servants to clean the silver)?

Of course, his dream-vision had libelled the excellent Mrs Whittingham, who would never have held such opinions, but it bore a rather close relationship to his own beliefs about what he thought such people were really like. If he thought they were frauds, it was because he was beginning to think the same thing about himself.

Could there really be a reactionary Caliban lurking in the mud at the bottom of his soul? Not Caliban, perhaps, but Uriah Heep, cringing and hand-wringing, backing into chairs and knocking over occasional tables. He had to live with this creature and hide its existence from Wanda. She was so candid in her judgments, so transparent in her motives, that you felt that for her the world was a sort of day-nursery: it only needed organizing and tidying up by good-hearted young women, and we'd all be winging our way to a millennium where nobody's nose or bottom would need wiping, ever again.

Poor Ted.

He had joined the Department of Social Sciences at Barmouth at a time of university expansion, which was also a period of violent unrest. A month or two after his arrival, a right-wing politician invited by the tiny Conservative Club had been prevented from speaking and spattered with scarlet paint. Ted's students regarded this as a great victory: we are not here to examine life, but to change it.

One of their tactics had involved jostling the politician's wife on her way back to the waiting car, and then hammering relentlessly on its roof while shouting, 'Tory, Fascist pig.' Through the car window she was seen to break down and become hysterical.

Cautious and self-serving, Ted did not join his colleagues and their students on the barricades. Apart from an occasional 'Right on!' he offered no open support. In spite of this the politician's wife took to putting in a regular appearance in his dreams.

Ted himself had only seen her on the local television news, but he had looked up the politician in *Who's Who*, had found that the wife's name was Angela, daughter of a landowner in some remote shire, and his unconscious had provided him with an arrogant horsey woman, unlikely to have succumbed to external stress. He was, however, using an old edition. The one who had wept in the limousine was the second wife, Deirdre. Until quite recently she had been the politician's secretary.

She appeared in his dreams in a large department store or a railway station. 'Hullo, Angela,' he said. 'Hello, Ted,' Deirdre-Angela answered, 'Are you still living with that idiotically ingenuous wife and those two conventional children in that common-looking house? Don't you ever have any fun?'

In another, worse dream he encountered her at a house party in one of those large and splendid houses he had seen when open to the public. This time he had been properly invited, people were being nice to him, he was not required to leave; in fact, they begged him to stay. Then suddenly Angela-Deirdre leaned out of a mullioned window and started mocking him: 'Ted, what are you doing here? You must go away now and join the students and workers.' Everybody began sneering at him, there was a high cachinnation all around him. He was naked on the lawn among the flowerbeds, trying to cover his genitals with his hands.

Heavily silent next morning, he avoided looking at Wanda. At the breakfast table he pushed Tamsin too hurriedly into her high chair, so that she started crying endlessly.

Poor Ted.

Towards the end of the academic year, his two oldest friends, members of his gang, Ned and Fred, came to stay, bringing their current girls. Wanda spent most of her time in the kitchen, either preparing casseroles or cleaning up after they had been eaten, and Fred's girl joined her there. Fred's girl sulked a good deal, feeling neglected and suspecting herself to be pregnant. She went on and on about this to Wanda, who missed a good deal of the narrative line; she had recently invested in a secondhand dishwasher, which gave off a heavy grumbling sound.

Ned's friend stayed behind with the men. She was a rather recent acquisition, a big lustrous girl with amused eyes. Quite unaware of what was expected of her, she interposed herself in their conversations in a way they found strangely unmannerly. Whenever they met, Ted, Ned and Fred fell into a discourse which was a sort of fugue on all the themes they had in common, full of humourless scoffing and a cynicism unearned by experience.

This time, it was true, there was a new topic to agree about. A Royal visit to the University was in the offing; already student committees were going round organizing a series of protest demonstrations.

Fred and Ned said: 'Bloody good thing, too. She's just a social parasite, in't she? I min, we're paying for her, you and me, right?'

Ted said: 'Right on.' He was pleased that in the five years since they'd come down from their university, Fred and Ned had kept the faith, though their lives had gone in somewhat differing directions. Fred had infiltrated the education department of a large and moribund London publisher; Ned was 'research assistant' to a Labour politician.

They had been drinking beer since five o'clock and it was now ten-thirty. 'Down with all Royal prostitutes,' they said.

Ned's girl said: 'You wouldn't talk like that if she was a man.'

The three of them turned to look at her.

'What woon't we say if she was a man, honey?' Ned asked. She was his but, like the others, he didn't seem to know her Christian name.

'Everything you've been saying, you lousy clots. You're getting at her not because she's Royal but because she's a woman. The Royal bit is just an excuse. You're all scared of women and you want to keep us in the kitchen. You're a bloody lot of pigs, who know fuck all about women, the lot of you. Fenella and Wanda and I could sort you out, if we wanted to.'

If they were appalled by this, they did not show it. Indeed, none of them said anything. The girl glared at them and went out of the room. More doors banged than seemed likely to exist in a house as small as this one. Upstairs, either Jake or Tamsin woke up and started crying.

Outside, in a night of rain and wind-shuddering privet hedges, they heard the car start up. This belonged to the nameless girl: the other visitors would have to return to London by train.

Ned, Ted and Fred sat silent, blurred by drink.

'Will she be all right?' Fred asked at last.

'She'll be all right,' Ned said. 'She's been driving since she was twelve. Round Daddy's estate.'

This seemed to dispose of the girl. 'We'd better move on to Scotch,' Ted said.

Poor Ted.

He slept that night with open, crusted mouth. All the same, he dreamed.

His dream was one of the exhausting kind that seems to occupy the entire night. At first it presented him with a sort of preview of the forthcoming visit: he marched linking arms with the sociology students, who carried placards reading 'Royals Out' and 'Cut Her Allowance'. And then suddenly he broke ranks, dashed forward and bowed to the visitor. Immediately it was night-time, they were at the Ball organized by the Vice-Chancellor but boycotted by students and faculty, and he was dancing with her, a small thickish figure, but with a perfect sun-gold complexion, and somehow spicy and succulent in appearance, like over-rich cake. In shrill ruling class tones, a voice long drained of concern or sympathy, she was ordering him to visit her on a tropical island. He accepted like a shot and woke up, smiling, before she could start humiliating him.

That morning, breakfast was late. It was Sunday, and the two women had already gone out with Jake and Tamsin. While Ned and Fred sneered over the newspapers, Ted sat in silence, feeling comfortable and happy. His unconscious mind kept betraying everything they all stood for, and it did not matter any more.

This is his final dream of unfair women. But he has another, recurring dream that takes him a long, long way into the future – exactly ten years, in fact. Ted and Wanda are still together, but there is a different light over everything. It is as though you had looked at your watch thinking it five in the morning, and found that it is really five in the afternoon.

And they don't live in Barmouth any more but in London: Fulham, to be precise, but very nearly Chelsea. Now that he is in Public Relations, Ted makes far more money than he did as a provincial academic. However, he has a mortgage and, what with stripping the pine staircase and rebuilding the roof, the house has involved them in endless costs that the surveyor had not foreseen. Both Jake and Tamsin are at boarding schools, where the fees are colossal and they need uniforms, and riding lessons are extra. Wanda has a fitted kitchen, with ceramic hobs and an almost silent dishwasher, but she still has her outside interests. For the moment, tax relief for private education ('We actually save the Government a lot of money') has taken over from a transitory concern with battered wives ('They invariably go back for more'). She meets a lot of the right people, and later she may stand for the local council as Conservative candidate.

And so life goes on. In their bedroom, with its long range of built-in wardrobes, Ted sleeps deeply and, beardless now of course, can easily face himself in his shaving-mirror. There are occasions when one seems to have a dream inside another dream. But, if this is the case with Ted, they are all of the type that one forgets at the very moment of awaking.